CW01236710

Soul Workout
keeping your spirit healthy

Janice Speddings

authorHOUSE®

AuthorHouse™ UK Ltd.
1663 Liberty Drive
Bloomington, IN 47403 USA
www.authorhouse.co.uk
Phone: 0800.197.4150

© 2013 Janice Speddings. All rights reserved.

No part of this book may be reproduced, stored in a retrieval system, or transmitted by any means without the written permission of the author.

Published by AuthorHouse 11/21/2013

ISBN: 978-1-4918-8486-7 (sc)
ISBN: 978-1-4918-8487-4 (e)

Image copyright belongs to Janice Speddings

This book is printed on acid-free paper.

Because of the dynamic nature of the Internet, any web addresses or links contained in this book may have changed since publication and may no longer be valid. The views expressed in this work are solely those of the author and do not necessarily reflect the views of the publisher, and the publisher hereby disclaims any responsibility for them.

Table of Contents

INTRODUCTION ix

PART ONE—PREPARING FOR
YOUR SOUL WORKOUT..................................1

Chapter 1—Could This Be For You? 3

Chapter 2—Getting Practical.....................................14

Chapter 3—Planning A Group Workout....................17
- *Setting The Event Up (Pre-Event)*
- *Preparing The Programme—
  Managing It On The Day*
- *Handy Checklist*

Chapter 4—Working Out Alone................................39

Chapter 5—Using 'Stations' Within A Workout 44
- *The Metaphor Explained*
- *Planning A Scripture Station*
- *Planning A Journalling Station*
- *Planning An Art Station*
- *Planning A Nature Station*

PART TWO—SO NOW YOU'RE READY TO WORKOUT 57

Chapter 6—In The Changing Room 59
- *The Metaphor Explained*
- *Suggested Exercises*
- *Notes For Group Leaders*

Chapter 7—Don't Neglect Your Warm Up 73
- *The Metaphor Explained*
- *Suggested Exercises*
- *Notes For Group Leaders*

Chapter 8—Cardiovascular Work 86
- *The Metaphor Explained*
- *Suggested Exercises*
- *Notes For Group Leaders*

Chapter 9—Weight Resistance 110
- *The Metaphor Explained*
- *Suggested Exercises*
- *Notes For Group Leaders*

Chapter 10—Flexibility And Balance 148
- *The Metaphor Explained*
- *Suggested Exercises*
- *Notes For Group Leaders*

Chapter 11—Cooling Down 172
- *The Metaphor Explained*
- *Suggested Group Exercises*
- *Suggested Exercise For Working Out Alone*

Chapter 12—Back In The Changing Room 183
- *The Metaphor Explained*
- *For Individuals*
- *Notes For Group Leaders*

PART THREE—LEAVING
THE WORKOUT BEHIND............................ 193

Chapter 13—Hanging On To
The Feel-Good Factor.. 195

POSTSCRIPT AND FINALLY....
A WORD OF THANKS 207

APPENDIX 1—Suggested Programmes
For Soul Workout Group Events....................... 209

APPENDIX 2—Suggested Reading
And On-Line Resources.................................. 213

APPENDIX 3—Seeking Spiritual
Accompaniment 219

About the Author 221

Introduction

The idea for 'Soul Workout' came as I daydreamed my way through a long bus journey from home to the gym. As I tried to work up a passion for my forthcoming exercise I began to see some connections between what I would be doing in my gym programme and the discipline of living out my Christian faith. Not an obvious connection, I grant, but as I pondered the metaphor, the more it seemed to fit.

I thought about it a lot over the following weeks and the more I came to understand the metaphor, the more I felt I wanted to share it. This desire has never left me. I have shared it in the form of Quiet Days at different venues but now I feel that the metaphor can be trusted enough to take to a wider audience—hence the writing of this book.

Not everyone will warm to the idea of exercise (physical or spiritual) nor easily connect a metaphor between exercise and the spiritual journey: indeed, I would have had no understanding of it myself at one time—and even less interest. However, we live in an age of heightened awareness of the problems of obesity and lethargy and the benefits to be gained from healthy eating and exercise. The call to exercise cries out from magazines and television programmes, to doctors' surgeries and physiotherapists' couches. We are frequently urged to be proactive about our health: to err on the side of prevention rather than cure.

So, in the spirit of being proactive about my health, I joined a gym in my forties.

What became obvious to me as I meandered through my bus-journey daydreams was that my gym regime also gave me a framework on which to work proactively on my *spiritual* health and wholeness. Out of my subsequent musings came the Quiet Days and out of them has come this book.

I anticipate that the structured approach of the Soul Workout will be most easily translated into a group setting and, in respect of this, the majority of **Part 1** will focus on a group approach. Church groups, faith groups and other communities seeking to deepen spiritual awareness may want to consider using the material in this book: maybe as a one-off event or maybe as a series of sessions.

Introduction

Leading such an event can be daunting, especially if you are not an experienced group leader and so I include a chapter giving basic information on how to organise, plan and run a Soul Workout Quiet Day as well as a handy checklist of materials and essentials for leaders.

Even when there are no plans to run a group event, the exercises can still be very useful tools for individual reflection. Though less likely to be used in as structured a framework when used individually, I can attest to the value of drawing on the material for personal quiet times. To honour this aspect of the work, I include a chapter at the end of Part 1 to help those who will be exercising alone.

Like all metaphors, Soul Workout has its limitations. It is not intended to be the definitive way to approach your spiritual life and, indeed, it may feel *too* structured for some people. It is offered as *one* way of checking out the state of your spiritual health from time to time. I encourage you, whether leading a group or having a go in the privacy of your own home, to pick out the parts that work for you and be the owner of them: adapt them, stretch them, translate them into something you can connect with. Above all, I ask that you allow God (however you relate to him) into that deepest part of yourself—the part we call the soul—and let him be your personal Fitness Instructor.

So, what *is* a soul workout?

We are all familiar with the notion that physical exercise helps to maintain healthy bodies. Cardiovascular, also known as aerobic, exercise encourages our hearts and lungs to work efficiently while weight resistance work enables us to strengthen muscles; floor exercises help us to maintain flexibility and balance.

The metaphor which began to crystallize in my mind enabled me to see clearly that these principles of heart-health, muscle strength and flexibility are just the same principles we need to sustain a healthy spiritual life. The difference is in the application.

Maintaining a healthy relationship with God is the equivalent of ***cardiovascular exercise***: freeing blockages from my prayer life, working at seeing God in every area of my life and being present to God's leading is what I seek. Above all, it is about the free-flow of love between us. Preserving a healthy spiritual heart, lungs and circulation doesn't come easily: it takes effort and energy.

Just like aerobic exercise.

But life has a habit of throwing lots of problems our way. Just as we think life is great and we are happy, something happens to upset our equilibrium. Tragedy, relationship problems, ill-health and other life events cause sadness,

Introduction

anger, disappointment, or anxiety. It can sometimes feel that life is all too much and we will never be happy again: we may feel unequal to the task of getting through the dark place and this leaves us feeling weak and vulnerable.

Just as ***weight resistance*** exercise helps us to build strong muscle, so, in spiritual terms, we need to build up and sustain an ability to cope with the pressures of life: through our relationship with God we are then enabled to work on strengthening our spiritual muscles. We become balanced and internally supple.

Dark days will still come but we will be stronger to face them.

Floor exercises help to tone our bodies, enabling us to maintain ***flexibility and balance***: these simple bend and stretch movements keep our limbs moving and supple. In just the same way, we need to keep spiritually flexed by maintaining a regular discipline of time with God.

A workout is good for the body. It is also good for the soul.

Is this book for me?

Soul Workout is written from a Christian perspective because that's where I'm coming from but it is not

Soul Workout

written from any particular denominational or rigid theological position.

If you can say 'yes' to any of the following statements then this book is for you:

- ➤ If you long to relate to God in a personal and real way;

- ➤ If you want to deepen your relationship with God, however you perceive him, and you want that relationship to influence the rest of your life;

- ➤ If you long to find God within His created world;

- ➤ If you want to deepen your reading of scripture and/or your prayer life, through the senses or through the use of art or your imagination;

- ➤ If you want to bring issues of your life to God in prayer in a way that is much more than a 'shopping list' of things you want God to do for you;

- ➤ If you want to check out how life is for you at the moment or gain new insights into your faith life;

- ➤ If you want to look at the balance of energy going in to your life against the energy of what you give out, *then this Soul Workout book is for you.*

Introduction

How to use this book

In order to get the most out of the book I suggest that you first decide whether you want to use it as a workbook for your personal faith journey or whether you are considering using it as a resource for group use.

Next, read the book from cover to cover: *if you only want it for personal use then feel free to skip over the parts connected with group use in Part One, but read everything else.* Reading Part Two will give you an overall view of the workout and is the equivalent of visiting the gym for the first time: you will be shown around, given an idea of what is on offer and you can then decide what you need and what exercise regime will work for you.

Part One will introduce you to the ideas and planning needed for setting up a Workout, with a separate chapter devoted to working as an individual rather than within a group: you will find some practical tips and things to consider for both group and personal use.

Part Two has chapters devoted to taking you through the steps of a Soul Workout. Each chapter is divided into three parts: the first part (the metaphor explained) aims to help you connect with the metaphor through teaching and anecdote while the second part (suggested exercise) offers suggestions on how to apply the principles to your own spiritual workout; the third part offers extra notes for group leaders.

Part Three aims to help you take what you have done in your workout into the rest of your life, so that it becomes integrated into your normal routine: for instance, work you have done in the Weight Resistance section is only helpful if it really does help you to cope with life in all its messiness. Learning to utilise and build on your fitness regime is an essential part of doing it—otherwise taking 'time out' becomes self-indulgent and self-centred. A workout aims to be reflected in different aspects of your life and you need to be able to hang on to the 'Feel-Good Factor' after your workout time has finished.

Reading the book is only the beginning. It offers the groundwork.

Appendix 1 offers some suggested programmes for Soul Workout events while the other two Appendices offer useful resources for the future.

And finally . . . . something about me

When I am reading a book I often wonder about the author and what impels him or her to write in a particular way. So, I offer you a potted history of my own journey through life:

Introduction

I grew up in a working class area of Sheffield and was brought up in a very close, loving family. Methodist by denomination, I went through Sunday School and took adult membership when I was sixteen years old.

After university, I began my professional career in the early 1970's as a Social Worker in Sheffield—a career I felt called to but which I was not destined to stay in for life.

1989 saw me leave my social work career behind to help set up Footprints Counselling Service with three others and in 2004 the two of us remaining became Footprints Connection—a name that retains our roots but acknowledges that life evolves. One thing led to another and, along with my colleague Kay, I went on to train in Spiritual Direction. This and other spirituality work now makes up the majority of my time at Footprints.

Life has continued in a very unremarkable way with mixtures of highs and lows. My highs included marriage and motherhood and my lows were often connected to loss—especially the early deaths of both my parents; yet the sudden death of my mother proved to be life-changing in more ways than one. It was through her death that I had a most profound experience of God—an experience that went towards giving me a deeper desire to attend to my inner soul life. Then, about twenty years ago, I discovered my creative side and learnt to paint and craft. I began to discover joy in the process of creation: this, too, has had a profound effect on my soul journey.

Writing has always been a part of who I am but I confined myself to writing for work or for my own eyes only until I began to work in the area of spirituality: now I share some of what I write and in this spirit I share the Soul Workout metaphor with you.

I don't think it is coincidence that my creative side began to emerge after I began to be drawn towards a quieter, more contemplative way of worshipping and experiencing God, nor does it stretch the point to say that this was also the period in my life when I began to recognise the importance of physical exercise. It seems that my forties were the time to explore many avenues of my life and discover a richer seam of experience both inside and out.

If asked, I describe myself as a 'non-religious Christian' simply because I do not want denomination or dogma to restrict my relationship with God. Although mainstream church and I parted company some years ago, I feel blessed to have been brought up anchored and rooted in the Christian tradition. It gave me the groundwork for my journey: the disciplines of reading Scripture and prayer have remained important to me but my church is not now confined to stone walls or denominations.

Introduction

If I follow any tradition now it is a contemplative one: Ignation, Celtic and Franciscan traditions influence me deeply as do family and community.

I believe that God is in all things and that relationship with God is everything. I also believe that God wastes nothing of my life and he can use every scrap of experience—good or bad—to help me relate to Him.

However, he never forces me and I am 50% of the relationship. Like any other relationship, it pays to put time and energy into getting to know him as intimately as I can (and I am the first to admit that this is easier said than done). Though I do not claim to do any more than muddle along in life like everyone else, it is implicit that my bond with him influences the way I live and how I relate to others.

There is another thing that is implicit in my faith journey—and in this book—and that is the maxim that 'all is gift': I believe that God gives out of his love to me; I don't earn it—I never can—so why strive for something I can never attain? Maybe my 'work' is to fully accept the love he so freely offers and to try to live in a way that honours his gift.

I tell you these things about myself because Soul Workout is not an academic book; it comes from within. What is written comes from my own experiences of God

Soul Workout

and life. It is to be used as a stepping-off point, from where you are encouraged to be proactive in your own search for inner health and wholeness.

You might be pleased to know that to do a Soul Workout you do not have to rush out and buy a leotard, trainers or sweat band. You need no treadmill, bike or weight machines and you will not get out of breath. Furthermore, I encourage you to have as many cups of tea or coffee as you like and I have no objection to a biscuit or two. You may do it all seated in an armchair if you wish—though it would be good if you could spend some time outside, if at all possible—but more on that later.

Use this book as a resource but make the workout your own: this is about *your* spiritual walk so go where the Spirit leads. And enjoy the journey.

Part One
Preparing for Your Soul Workout

CHAPTER 1
Could This Be For You?

Anyone who knows me from the past will be extremely surprised that anything to do with 'workouts' should even enter my mind: I was never noted for my love of physical exercise in my younger life. I must confess that my school career was not without blemish in this respect: I bunked off Games whenever I could. It was only decades later that I began to see the benefit of keeping my heart, circulation and muscles in good working order. But better late than never!

My re-acquaintance with Gym began when I was just into my forties. It's a familiar story: too little exercise combined with a love of good food brought me to my mid-life crisis. I decided to take action . . . .

I had my ears pierced. Well, it took courage! And I love wearing earrings. But it did nothing for my health!

Soul Workout

It took about eighteen months of delaying tactics: I persuaded myself that running up and down stairs at work was enough exercise for a woman of my age. But the truth was somewhat different—the real reason I was delaying was that I was crippled with fear: fear of making a fool of myself, of injuring myself or of having a heart attack. This fear was so strong that, every time I psyched myself up to go into the ladies-only gym I passed every day on my way to work, I chickened out.

When I finally walked through the door and said, 'I want to join' it was almost a relief.

It would be untrue to say I have always loved it, for Gym and I have a love-hate relationship. It would also be untrue to say that I have gone three times a week since then.

Indeed, when that gym closed down I had a couple of years without going anywhere.

But my health suffered.

I then joined another gym (the one that gave me my Soul Workout daydreams) but that didn't work out too well and so I came to my third, and present, gym. It's a small place in a retirement village near to where I live and is open to the local community; a 'liquorice allsorts' gym where residents in trousers held up with braces workout at their own pace by the side of strapping young blokes running on the treadmill with sweat pouring out of them.

Me?

I go with my daughter. Sometimes it's hard graft and sometimes we're up for it. If we have time, we treat ourselves to the spa and steam room afterwards.

Sometimes we can't be bothered to go!

The hardest thing about doing a workout at a gym is getting there!

I can always think of a hundred and one reasons why I can't possibly go that day. Any excuse suffices as long as it means I don't have to face the rigours of the workout: my back twinges; I haven't got time; I didn't sleep well; I haven't got the energy.

Why am I telling you all this? Because getting down to a Soul Workout is no different.

If any of the following excuses sound familiar, then we're on the same wavelength:

> I haven't got time;
> I'm not in the right frame of mind;
> What if I don't get anything from it?

Soul Workout

> I don't know where to start (so I'll not);
> I've got to get this work done first;
> I'll just make this phone call;
> I *promise* I'll do it tomorrow (or next time).

The *good* news is that God knows all our excuses—and still loves us. The *bad* news is that workouts will always require effort. They won't happen on their own. We need motivation.

Getting Motivated

My thesaurus offers the following words for motivation:

Incentive; inspiration; drive; enthusiasm; impetus; stimulus; spur; driving force.

I don't know about you, but these words sound like hard work. Whether we're talking about physical workouts or spiritual ones, motivation doesn't come easily.

My motivation levels rise and fall like tidal waves: from being high-tide 'raring to go' (infrequent) to low-tide 'I'm forcing myself' (most often), I have to make an effort. Many times I have dodged the issue by getting caught up in other things until, what a surprise! I no longer have time to get to the gym, do a workout and then get to work.

Then the guilt starts: 'I should have made more of an effort'; 'I'm my own worst enemy'; 'I waste too much time'.

The guilt makes my stress levels rise and I feel rubbish for the rest of the day. That night I don't sleep well. The following day I *really* feel too tired to face a workout!

I'm sure you see a pattern emerging.

It's no different with a Soul Workout: there is always something else to do and then the opportunity is gone. All you're left with are good intentions and guilt.

The only way to break this cycle is to make sure that you are truthful with yourself.

Sometimes there are valid reasons why you can't do a workout: having a dodgy tummy does not lend itself to strenuous exercise. Likewise, knowing you have to leave for an important appointment in half an hour is enough of a valid reason to not begin a spiritual workout.

Whether it is in a group or alone, the best reason for doing a Soul Workout is because *you want to*. If, having read this book, you want to dive in and have a go then your motivation will be high. But remember that if you need to get a group together and plan an event, it isn't going to happen for a while. Let the planning and preparation for the event fuel your motivation.

Soul Workout

On an individual level you may be able to sort out a chunk of time fairly quickly but, if not, don't leave it too long or you might find that your motivation has taken a dive.

To help keep motivation high, work out what is drawing you to this metaphor: is it about wanting to spend quality time with God instead of the rushed shopping list of a prayer you offer him each day? Is it because you feel 'stuck' in your spiritual life and want to find some refreshment or freshness in approach? Perhaps you have a decision to make and you want to bring it before God so that you can discern which way to go. All these are valid reasons for getting into a Workout but they are not exhaustive: there are many reasons, not least of which is a desire for stillness and quiet.

There are, however, not so good reasons . . . .

Be careful of phrases like 'I *should* do it' or 'it will be good for me' or 'my housegroup is doing it' or (worst of all) 'the vicar says I ought to do it'. None of these are motivating statements. If you undertake a workout in this frame of mind you will, at best, get little from it. At worst, you will subtly and often unconsciously, sabotage it. Your mind will stray, you will be critical of the material and yourself, you will pretend that it's great on the surface but, deep down, you will be resentful of the time it takes.

Could This Be For You?

While 'ought' and 'should' are not good reasons for a Soul Workout perhaps you can spend some time getting to the bottom of where they come from: are they words from your past? From authority figures (past or present)? Do these words form a significant part of other areas of your life?

It may be that you uncover something important by asking yourself these questions. Any new-found awareness may be enough to move you on in your journey—and, in that case, Soul Workout has already played an important role in your life.

It may be that you recognise that you need some help to move you on. At the back of this book you will find information about seeking Spiritual Direction (sometimes known as Spiritual Accompaniment) and about the Retreat Movement. Spiritual Directors can act in the same way as personal trainers in a gym; they can offer information, suggestions, encouragement and support when the going gets tough.

If you want to increase your motivation, learn to 'say it as it is'. If you can recognise that you are making excuses then ask yourself 'why?' . . . .

Paula had been invited to a Soul Workout Quiet Day *organised through her church.* Her best friend was going but Paula came up with the following reason to opt out:

Soul Workout

'I'm just no good at that sort of thing: I'm always afraid I'm going to get a fit of the giggles or my stomach is going to rumble at the quietest moment and I'll show myself up. Besides, I'm not into all that meditation stuff—I'd probably fall asleep and end up snoring. You're more academic than me: I'm just an idiot'.

Fear of being shown up as inferior can be de-motivating.

Paula stayed away but felt annoyed with herself as she recognised the root of her excuses was a lack of confidence. Had she been able to say 'I've never done anything like this before and I'm not sure how I'll take to it, but I'll give it a go' the outcome may have been different.

Julie had set aside a morning to do a Soul Workout. But on the morning in question she found herself having this internal battle:

'I need to make this phone call while I think about it—I might forget later.'

'But I can always write myself a note to remind me.'

'I'm only making this phone call so that I'll not have enough time to get down to my Soul Workout. I just can't get motivated.'

'Why don't I want to do it?'

'It might touch a raw nerve and I'll end up crying.'

'What's the raw nerve?

'I'm not sure where I am with God. And my family are driving me nuts. I'm a bad mother.'

'I really need to sort myself out. I never get time to myself. I never get time to listen to God—*if h*e's there!'

'But the Soul Workout will give me that time. I cleared my morning so that I could do it. Now I'm filling it up again with jobs that can be done later.'

'I could make a cup of tea and sit down with my Bible and see where it goes. If I get into 'stuff' I don't want to do then I don't have to do it. Nobody is making me do anything. Not even God.'

'Yes. I'll do it because I *want* to.'

Understanding what was going on below the surface helped Julie to be motivated to do her workout.

Choice as a Motivator

In the second scenario above, it would seem that Julie was initially feeling some kind of internal pressure to do the workout. She said she just couldn't get motivated.

Soul Workout

There's a sense of wasting time as the phone call could be made later. Perceived coercion is very de-motivating.

She reasoned that she had a choice and that the phone call wasn't the actual reason she was delaying. As she worked through to the root of her excuses she reached a point where she could say, 'I'll see where it goes.' Julie was beginning to be motivated by recognising that she had choices.

Feeling that she was not being coerced or pressurised changed her perspective into 'I'll do it because I want to.' If she found herself dealing with 'stuff' that made her feel uncomfortable, then she would have a decision to make: to carry on or shift gear. It would be her choice.

She may *need* to get into 'stuff' and may well find that looking at it within the workout is just the thing that will help her. But the choice is hers—not even God will make her do it if she doesn't want to.

Feeling free to *not* deal with issues is strangely empowering and often helps us to be strong enough to tackle them. Choice can be motivating.

'Time out' as a Motivator

Another way of motivating yourself is to see it as 'time out': Not quite a pampering session, it's true, but it can be a relaxing and peaceful experience. It needn't be hard work. Indeed, much of the cardiovascular work may actually be about allowing God to speak through the quietness, maybe through nature or pictures—but more about that in the chapter on 'Stations'.

This is where the metaphor of a workout doesn't work so well: physical workouts always involve some part of you being on the move. With a Soul Workout I encourage you to be still for much of the time and to allow God to work *in* you.

Whether you plan to lead a group, be a participant or do the workout alone, you need to be motivated. The biggest motivator of all is the feel-good factor available from spending quality time with God and with your inner self.

Convinced yet?

Chapter 2
Getting Practical

When Soul Workout has been used as a Quiet Day, there has been a combination of group time, when I have explained and expanded the metaphor to the whole group, alongside long periods of silence, when participants are encouraged to work on their own. A variety of indoor and outdoor 'stations' have helped to resource and supply ideas for getting into the work in the form of reflective exercises.

Whether the workout is approached as a group or in an individual setting the process remains the same.

It is best to follow the order suggested in each chapter; it may seem unnecessary to labour the point but the sequence is important. Hopefully, your initial reading will help you to get a feel of the wholeness of the workout and so begin to see the possibilities for your group or yourself.

Getting Practical

It may not be possible to have the luxury of a whole day so you may need to employ a 'mix and match' process to fit whatever time you have. *But I encourage you to be as committed to the Warm Up and Cool Down exercises as to the rest.* In physical workouts these gentle exercises prevent muscular pulls and strains; it may seem strange to think that they may be relevant in a spiritual sense, but they are! They help to focus your attention away from distracting thoughts and outer stresses and into your inner 'soul' life and then, at the end of your workout, re-focus you back into the outer world and those things you need to attend to.

Plan your time so that you will be able to do the workout you want: this is more difficult for individuals working out at home than for a group who will already have set aside a chunk of time. Planning and preparation are crucial to a smooth workout so don't be tempted to 'wing it'. I have included some pointers to help you in the chapters devoted to groups and personal workouts.

Plan your venue so that you have space and privacy: this is something I will talk more on in the coming chapters but suffice it to say here that the venue can make or destroy the workout. There is nothing harder than trying to be quietly reflective in the next room to a children's party or near to the thud-thud of blaring pop music.

Soul Workout

Make sure you have what you need beforehand (all gyms have equipment!): a notebook and pen are basic equipment for a workout (whether in a group or not) and as a Christian, I would also include a Bible. If you want to use other items to help focus your time then the chapter on using Workout Stations will give you some ideas. In terms of practicalities, I have offered basic and advanced exercises in each section to take account of different levels of experience.

The only other thing you need is a willingness to have a go.

Of course, there are no guarantees, but my own experience of workouts (of both the physical and spiritual kind) is that there is a feel-good factor to be had on completion of them: the time and energy you have invested will translate into feeling stronger, more rested and closer to God, others and yourself.

Though I hope to encourage your progress through the pages of this book, the work remains yours. It takes personal effort and a degree of commitment but the results can be truly valuable. Try it and see.

Chapter 3
Planning A Group Workout

Aerobics classes are popular ways to exercise and they come in many guises: from Keep Fit to Zumba, Step-aerobics to Salsa, these classes offer something attractive to many people. It isn't that they are soft options because they are often hard, sweaty work—even if they are done to music. The attraction is often that people (especially women) see such classes as helping to keep them on the straight and narrow of exercise: they are somewhere to go with friends; they offer a sharing environment—somewhere to share the struggles *and* the triumphs—with people who will support and encourage because they are equally involved.

Classes are led by a Fitness Instructor but members of the group offer mutual support as the class stretches and bends its way through the programme. Often the support is non-verbal: a look here, a nod there; a groan from one participant may evoke an understanding smile from a next door neighbour.

Running a Soul Workout Group can be the same.

First of all, many people find it easier to make time for a group activity—for them, doing a workout in the privacy of their own home just doesn't hit the spot: maybe they will be too easily distracted and find that time has gone and they have done very little except feel guilty that they've wasted time.

Or, maybe they don't know how to really get into it: there are those who are naturally followers rather than leaders and, for them, reading this book may be fine but they will still struggle to know how to put it all together as a programme for themselves. Leaders can pull a programme together from the resources offered in this book.

If you feel drawn towards running a Soul Workout Group you need to consider a few basic things first:

- *Who is the workout for?* Is it for yourself and one or two close friends? Or are you looking to cast the net wider and advertise the event at church, within your locality or wider? It is important to recognise that setting a group up and being responsible for it changes the dynamic of your involvement: this isn't to say you cannot participate and get something valuable from the session but the nature and extent of your personal

Planning A Group Workout

participation will be affected by the degree of your involvement in the organisation of it.

- *Who would be leading it?* Would you want to lead it by yourself or find someone else to lead with you?

  If the workout is for you and a very small group of close friends, then maybe you could each lead a section of the day: as long as you are clear about who is going to do what, this model can work well and enables each one of you to be a full participant as well as a leader.

  If, however, you are looking at the workout as something to offer to a wider group, you need to be clear about your role as leader. People who book on to a day like this are often unsure what to expect and can be nervous as they begin; they need a leader, or leaders, to be calm, confident and clear—even if that's not how you are feeling inside!

  To share leadership is to share the load and support each other. It also means that you may be able to participate more fully in the parts you are not actually leading.

- *What are you hoping to achieve through doing the workout?* Is it to try something new? To deepen your own prayer-life? To help deepen someone else's prayer-life? A combination of these things?

Don't attempt to get a group together unless you are clear about why you want to do it—any lack of clarity will show up as a woolly presentation, confusing and disappointing participants. If your main aim is personal (perhaps to try out new ways of praying or meditating) then don't offer it to a wider group. It would be better to stick to a few close friends where you can support each other.

If, however, you are committed to leading a wider group it is essential that you first have a good working knowledge of all the elements of the workout: it is difficult to have a successful outcome if the leader is unfamiliar with the content.

- *Would you want to offer a full day or only a portion of it? A one-off event or a series of sessions?* Deciding this at the beginning will help you to decide on a sensible programme: it's as bad to cram too much in as to not have enough. If you decide you can only do a morning, or an afternoon then adjust the programme accordingly. When I have run Soul Workout as a full day I have given the morning over to

Planning A Group Workout

the warm up and cardiovascular exercises. As will be explained in the chapters relating to them, this eases the participant into the day and focuses attention on the importance of deepening relationships with God. The afternoon has centred on weight resistance (bearing our burdens), flexibility and balance, followed by the cool down. All of these terms will be explained as you read through the book.

I have, however, offered 'Mini' Soul Workouts as afternoon or evening meetings when I have concentrated on cardiovascular exercises—but including a short warm up and cool down as well. It is important that you have this period of easing in and letting go.

Alternatively, if time is limited, you may decide to divide your programme to include one cardiovascular exercise and one weight resistance exercise: still a Mini workout but includes shorter periods of all the elements.

Remember that not everyone can commit to a full day and it is difficult for a group to have people coming and going at different times. **You need to decide what you will offer and stick with it.** Appendix 1 will give you some ideas on putting a programme together, whatever the length of your proposed event.

- *Will you be responsible for all aspects of organisation?* If you are offering the Soul Workout specifically to a group (rather than just a few of you getting together), there are many practical issues to deal with. As well as putting the programme together and leading it on the day there are many other jobs needing attention.

It can be a lot of hard work for one person and it is good to work alongside others. However, it is worth taking into account that people work differently: some like to be organised and make sure everything is in place in plenty of time while others work better under pressure and at the last minute. Find out how your co-leaders work and make sure you are clear about who is doing what and when.

Once you have decided to go ahead with putting on a Soul Workout event you need to begin planning: some of you may be experienced group leaders so I have included a quick handy checklist at the end of this chapter to help you cover all bases but for those of you who are not experienced or confident in organising and running an event I have written a more extensive explanation below.

Planning A Group Workout

What you need to consider and plan for . . .

It can sound daunting to put an event together from scratch but many of the arrangements are a mixture of common sense and methodical planning, so don't be put off. Just because you will be leading doesn't mean to say you can't get enjoyment, satisfaction and much that is valuable from the event.

Preparation takes two distinct forms: *setting the event up*
managing the programme on the day

Setting the event up

In order to maximise the outcome of your event there are a number of things to consider and deal with long before the day arrives. Give yourself plenty of time to organise everything adequately but, above all, enjoy the planning as well as the event itself.

Thinking about numbers: a Soul Workout can work well for six to twenty people but there are several factors to take into account before rushing in. First and foremost, consider how many people you would feel comfortable in leading: if you are not used to leading groups then you may feel happier to go small in terms of numbers. A group of six people is a lovely size to work with if you are a little unsure but, if you feel confident and the venue allows it, then look at hosting a larger group.

The venue needs to offer the facilities you require for your event: It may be that you want to run the Workout from a venue well known to you—your church, local school or community centre. If you know the name of the person responsible for taking room bookings then sorting out dates, times and rooms is likely to be reasonably easy and stress-free. If you don't, then you will have to do a little detective work first: is there a notice-board or information on a website to help you? Do you know anyone who might be able to point you in the direction of the information you need?

- Before booking, make sure you have an idea of the size of group you are looking for and what amount of space you require. (Alternatively, you may decide to book the room and then let the numbers and programme be dictated by those parameters).

  If using a community-based venue is not possible or desirable you may want to look further afield and widen your search. Other possibilities may be larger city churches, or retreat centres (see Appendix for more information), hotels or even function rooms at pubs.

- The costs are likely to be far more substantial but sometimes these venues can offer facilities, such as catering, power-point and sound systems not

Planning A Group Workout

available at smaller venues: it all depends on who you are aiming the event at and how you want to run the day. Ask for information about costs and don't book without working out how this will affect what you intend to charge: see ***costs*** below.

- Larger venues usually require plenty of notice and you may find yourself having to book for the following year: the days I have run have been booked more than a year in advance as the Spirituality centre puts its programme together well in advance. Don't be put off if this is the case: it leaves you more time to firm up on all other aspects of the event.

- *Many venues will require a deposit at the time of booking.*

Costs: it is impossible to run an event without accruing some costs and so you need to work out how much you will charge each person for attending. Most people these days expect to pay something but the question of money doesn't always sit comfortably with us as leaders.

In order to know what to charge you need information about several things:

o   How much will the venue cost in total? Check that there will be no hidden costs, such as extra

Soul Workout

charges for the use of equipment or the car park. Don't forget to include any deposit in your figures.

o Will there be any catering costs? Even tea and coffee come at a price.

o Will you have to buy any materials, such as paper / art materials etc?

o Will you need to photocopy anything? Handouts? Resource materials? What are they likely to cost?

Will there be any costs attached to publicity? Word of mouth is fine if you are running a small group for your church but if you are looking at a larger event then you will need to publicise it: see ***publicity*** below.

o What about your own costs? Will you require payment for travel? Will you be looking to take a fee for your work? Many people don't but, if you are doing this as part of your work, you may feel you need to make a charge for your services.

o Are there be any other miscellaneous charges not accounted for above?

Planning A Group Workout

Don't be frightened by all this talk of costs—it really boils down to common sense and is less daunting than it sounds. Get as much information as you can about each of these factors; add up all the costs together and divide by the number of people you are looking to attract. That will give you your total charge. *Is this a realistic figure? Would YOU pay that much to go on the day?*

If the answer is 'no' then you need to readjust your plans. Is the venue too expensive? Do you need to look round for somewhere cheaper? Can you compromise with packed lunches instead of outside caterers? Do you really need to buy art materials or do you know anyone who could donate some felt tips and old wallpaper (the back of wallpaper rolls is wonderful for using in this way. Backing wallpaper can be very cheap to buy and you would only need one roll). Keep working on it till you get a figure that works.

When you have reached a reasonable charge and you are satisfied with the venue then book it before the price goes up!

Once you have begun to publicise the event you will not be able to change your prices so do your homework first and stick to the charge you come up with.

Publicity: these days there are a number of cheap ways to publicise events. Word of mouth, church notices, community notice boards, libraries and local shops are the traditional ways but these days local online forums, Facebook and Twitter also provide cheap and effective means of publicity (though these can be problematic if you are not computer literate). You may want to print out some leaflets to send to churches and / or other groups in your area. You may want to take out an advert in your local paper or advertise on local radio. If you can get a local paper to write an article about your planned event then that will help to get your event noticed. All these are good ideas but check the prices and also how much notice is needed for printing or broadcasting. Include all these costs in your pricing totals.

Publicity is easy if you are running a small, local event—maybe just at church or for a small group of local churches. Publicity only becomes more of an issue when you are planning a more detached event for individuals who do not already have a group identity and who have to be drawn together specifically for the event.

Whatever kind of event you are planning, try to make your leaflets or posters eye-catching. *Your publicity needs to contain enough information to whet the appetite without being too wordy and make sure that it has all relevant information about dates, times, venue, cost, contact and booking arrangements: strange at it may seem, these very obvious pieces of information are easily omitted and only noticed after printing is completed.*

Planning A Group Workout

Booking: If there is more than one person involved in planning, make sure you designate one specific person or one point of contact where people can get further information and / or book. To have different people taking bookings can cause difficulties in managing numbers and can lead to uncertainty and stress. Much better to agree who will be responsible and how bookings are to be taken:—

- Will people pay a deposit or pay in full when booking?

- How can they pay? Cash / cheque / card?

- What information do you need for contact details?

- Will you give receipts and confirm the booking?

All this may seem trivial and mundane but if you are planning an event where people need to book a place it is essential to have made these decisions.

Preparing the programme—Managing it on the day

Once you have decided on *when; where;* and *how many*, then you need to turn your attention to '*how*'. You need to think about what you see as the aims of the day, how long your Workout will last and what will be the physical limitations of the space you have.

Appendix 1 offers some Programme suggestions designed for different session lengths.

Managing the programme on the day will be easier if you have prepared well. Below you will find suggestions and things to think about for each section of the workout. It is not an exhaustive list but I hope you will find it useful as a starting point for your own preparations. The suggestions have been worded to help you think about how it may be on the day: trying to visualise the event in this way can be very helpful in making sure you have as many angles covered as possible before the event.

Before working on your detailed preparations *you need to have read **Part Two** of this book so that you know what each of the sections refers to.*

In the changing room:

- Prior to the group's arrival you need to have prepared the room and have any handouts, materials etc. ready so as not to delay the start of the day. You need to be fully conversant with the flow of the programme so that participants

Planning A Group Workout

feel that they are being held safely. No matter how you are feeling inside it is important for the group that you show a calm and confident exterior

- Make the most of the space available to you and try to bring a sense of peace and calm into your room arrangement. Having a circle or semi-circle of chairs around a simple visual display invites people in to the group space: a straight row may not be so appealing. Be led by your own instincts but remember that first impressions count for a lot.

- Will you greet people in the room/s you will be working in or somewhere else (reception, coffee area)? Do you want them to gather informally over coffee or filter into the room quietly as they arrive? This is their bridge between the ordinary routine of life and the Workout and it is likely that they will have some uncertainties and anxieties about the day. How you greet them is important.

- Once you have the group assembled and in their seats you may need to give out a few notices: location of toilets, catering arrangements and sometimes even the fire procedures (you need to acquaint yourself with these beforehand). If you will be using a few different rooms it will be helpful for people to know where to find you should they have a problem. Doing this now frees up the day and allows the programme to proceed without disruption. Keep any notices brief and to the point.

Don't neglect your Warm up: This is the first exercise the group will be doing and it is important that they are eased into it. In some circles this exercise is known as '*stilling*' as it is the place where the process of stilling the mind and body begins. The chapter will give you a few ideas on how to put the elements together to make the exercise meaningful so it does not need repeating here. However, if you are intending to use music, pictures or other items then make sure you have them ready and set up beforehand. Being prepared on the day takes away much of the stress!

Cardiovascular, Weight Resistance and Flexibility Work: At these points your group will be working on their own: these aspects of the day are very personal and people will appreciate their own space; they are likely to want to move from the group area into a more private, even secluded spot. This is where your choice of venue is really important and you need to have thought through the issue of space long before the day. If you only have one room, you may be able to rearrange the chairs so that they face away from each other—perhaps facing a

Planning A Group Workout

wall with a simple visual display such as a piece of cloth with a picture and candle standing on it (being mindful of the hazards of candles). Work out the positioning of the chairs beforehand and then moving them can be done quickly and with minimal disruption.

Having the use of different rooms (and maybe some outside space) means that people will sort themselves out in their own time. As long as they know where to find everything and are aware of the timetabling of the day then you can let them move into their personal work at their own pace. It will be helpful for them to know where you can be found, should they have a problem.

For each unit I have suggested the possible use of four different 'Work Stations'—Art, Nature, Scripture and Journaling: I suggest you make some early decisions about *if, what* and *how* such stations can be used on your day. If you only have one room then having an Art Station or a Nature Station may not be realistic whereas having the use of several rooms may lend itself to these ideas more readily. Decide *what, how much* and *where to locate* your resources according to the programme you are building. Then, give the group space and time to do their individual work—that's why they have signed up!

Cool Down: It is important that you, as leader, can offer an opportunity at the end of the day for individuals

Soul Workout

to regroup. Building in a group cool down exercise enables two things to happen: most importantly it gives everyone a way to 'let go' of the day in a constructive and affirming way; secondly it enables them to harness the supportive spirit of the group at a time when they will probably be tired and ready to finish. Although they will have been engaged in their own work for the majority of the time they will still have been aware of others around them so being able to end their workout within the group is very supportive.

Don't rush this exercise but give plenty of time for people to reflect on what they have been doing so that they can take away what has been useful and leave the rest behind. You might want to encourage each person to share a word (not a sentence, which is too lengthy) to summarise what the day has meant for them. This works best if you leave the invitation open for people to share if they want to—resist the temptation to go round the circle. It only puts people on the spot and can ruin the day for some. Be sure to tell people that it's okay not to share if they don't want to.

Back in the Changing Room: Most people need a bridge to get them back into the outside world, just as much as they needed one earlier to enter the world of the workout. Some may be wanting to hang on to the sense of peace and calm they are feeling as the workout draws to a close while others may be anxious about time and outside commitments. The most important thing to remember is to finish on time with a definite ending: don't let it fizzle out so that people are unsure whether or not they can leave. Depending on the group, you may feel it is appropriate to finish with a short prayer or Blessing but, if not, then a simple 'thank you for coming and have a safe journey home' will do the job.

Be sure to stay around for a while, just in case someone wants to speak to you but don't get drawn into lengthy conversations. You will probably be as tired as anyone else and still have the room to sort out so, if necessary, politely excuse yourself. An acquaintance of mine, when faced with a number of people all wanting her attention, cleverly employed their help to tidy up as they talked. They all went away satisfied!

By being well prepared in the planning and running of the Soul Workout you will not only offer participants a valuable day full of opportunity but it is likely that you will take away a sense of achievement and satisfaction yourself. Take the Soul Workout to your heart and the journey from planning to delivery will form part of your own faith journey.

Use the checklist below to remind yourself of things to do.

Soul Workout

Handy Checklist

Setting the event up

- Will you be working alone or with co-leaders?

- If you are working with others, what will your specific roles be?

- What size group are you looking to work with?

- Have you found a suitable venue?

- Have you worked out a suitable cost for the event?

- How are you publicising the event?

- How will bookings and payment be managed?

- Who will lead on the day?

- Does anything else need to be considered?

Preparing the Programme—Managing it on the day.

- If you are providing refreshments, don't forget to ask people about their dietary requirements. Organise any catering you require in plenty of time.

Planning A Group Workout

o   If you will be using equipment for music or presentation purposes make sure they are available and you know how to work them before the day arrives.

o   Prepare any handouts and / or programmes you intend to use throughout the day—making sure you have enough copies to go round.

o   Decide what 'Work Stations', visual displays, music etc. you intend to use and gather any materials you require. Further information and suggestions for workstations are given in Chapter 5.

o   Collect basic equipment such as notebooks, pens and Bibles (if appropriate) for the group or make sure participants know to bring their own.

o   Prepare the room(s) in a welcoming way before the arrival of any participants. Take into account any rearrangements of furniture you may need to make during the day to accommodate the programme.

o   Make sure you are fully conversant with the programme before the day starts.

o   Check any notices you may have and give them out at the start of the day. Make people aware of

Soul Workout

>   where they can find you during the day if there is a problem. Remind them to respect individuals' space and silence.

o   If you are planning to have any kind of sharing between participants (not necessary but some people prefer to) please remind everyone to respect confidentiality.

o   Make sure you have made people aware of the timings and progression of the programme.

o   Start on time and finish on time.

o   Enjoy both the preparation and the running of your event.

Chapter 4
Working Out Alone

It isn't always possible or desirable to get a group together for a workout but that doesn't mean to say that you can't make use of the resources of this book. Just as physical exercise can be done alone, so can a Soul Workout—and it requires less planning than a group event.

But it does need *some* planning: this chapter offers the chance to think through how an individual workout can be used to the best advantage. The metaphor and exercises in Part Two can then be used in a way appropriate to your situation.

First of all you need to think about why you want to use the metaphor? What draws you to it?

Do you find you have a natural connection to the image it conjures up or will you have to work at making the connection?

Soul Workout

Don't be tempted to skip the symbolism of the image so that you can get to the exercises quicker: in order to truly understand *why* you are doing a workout you need to understand the metaphor and the process.

Do you have experience of contemplative reflection or are you going into unknown territory?

If it will be a new experience take a moment to ask yourself 'how am I feeling about it?'

Next, you need to think through, and plan, a chunk of time that will not have any interruptions or outside demands. A day is ideal but you can get by with a morning or afternoon. If that is still impractical then try to put aside an hour. Obviously you will need to adjust the exercises to the amount of time available: don't try to do too much. This is where putting some thought into planning and preparation is helpful.

Be realistic and plan around the time you know you will have. Rushing, being late for something else or trying to multitask will not work. This needs to be quality 'ring-fenced' time that doesn't detract from anything else. Spending half an hour doing one of the exercises is far more valuable than trying to fit two or three into the time; ending your workout fifteen minutes before the family are due home is far more beneficial than cramming in the extra time and then being harassed by them arriving home five minutes early.

Deciding *where* to do your workout may or may not be an issue but before deciding, think about a few options:

Being at home may work well for you but, as I know only too well, it can be very easy to get side-tracked. It may not seem like a big deal to put a load of washing on, or make a quick phone call but it can disturb your concentration, divert your focus—however briefly—and make it difficult to get back on track.

If you think this may happen to you, then doing your workout away from the washing machine and the phone may well solve the problem. Alternative venues can be varied. The following are offered as possible suggestions—

- ➢ If you go to a church you may be able to use space there—but don't make any assumptions: make sure you check with the person responsible for booking rooms.

- ➢ Some time ago, a friend offered me the use of her house for meditation while she was at work. Have you a friend who might be able to offer something similar? (be careful: if your friend will be in the house the temptation to chat can defeat the object. You both need to be really disciplined about not getting into conversation—if you both agree to this then your friendship will not suffer and I'm sure you'll not miss out on anything!)

- ➤ If you are within easy reach of the countryside you can take your workout in the fresh air: many people feel closer to God away from rooms and signs of modern living.

- ➤ Dotted all over the country there are retreat houses and spirituality centres. Some have facilities for day visitors wanting their own space. You would need to check on availability and cost.

Wherever you are, make sure that your mobile phone is switched off and your ipod is unavailable. Remember, this is your day and time for yourself and God.

Having made these plans, you need to decide what materials you want to use to make your workout special. There are no hard and fast rules but try to be imaginative as well as practical.

Working Out Alone

The basics are a pen and notebook but you might want to use a bible, music, pictures, art materials or other items: there are some suggestions in the next chapter.

Remember that whatever materials you want to use they are only a means to an end: it is better to stick to one or two items you feel will be really useful than to over-complicate matters.

Chapter 5
Using 'Stations' Within A Workout

In order to explain the importance of workstations I need to take you into the metaphor . . . .

Treadmills, bikes, rowing machines, mats, gym-balls, dumb-bells, and a variety of weight-resistance machines are the furniture of all gyms and are known as 'stations'. The gym I go to is small and only has a few stations but some gyms boast many: one gym I pass on the way to work boasts '147 stations'—too big for me!

Gym stations enable you to work hard by providing structure and focus to your exercise.

When I'm on the treadmill or bike I focus on getting a rhythm going—and, although I'm not a fan of most modern music, the music on the inevitable TV allows me to get into pace. I need a rhythm that allows me to work hard while remaining manageable: going for a stroll on the treadmill is not much use but equally I don't want the machine to go so fast it catapults me off the end.

The same is true of weight machines: I need to be able to work my muscles without ending up on the physiotherapist's table.

The secret is to go just above what is comfortable: if you're comfortable then you are not working hard enough but if you can't get your breath, and you are feeling faint or in pain then you are trying too hard.

And not all machines are suitable for everyone. There are some weight resistance machines I can't go on these days, as my knees no longer take the strain.

It's all about knowing your levels, pacing yourself but not getting lazy or complacent.

When I run the Soul Workout Quiet Days I like to provide four 'Stations' to enable participants to work hard in a way that will be beneficial to them: it must never be work that is imposed. To get the best from the day, each person needs to challenge themselves to move out of their comfort zone but, equally important, to find a focus and work at a pace and rhythm they can keep up with.

Balance, pace and rhythm are all important and are personal.

Sometimes noticing preferences but being prepared to have a go at something new can bring freedom and release from blocks and barriers. *The use of stations can help and encourage this process.*

If you are doing a Workout alone, it is highly unlikely that you will use 'stations' in the same way (just as you are unlikely to have a fully equipped gym at home): you are more likely to gather materials around you in a more casual way. Some of the material in this chapter will, therefore, not be relevant but I encourage you to read the ***Materials Suggestion List*** at the end of each 'station' section to give you some ideas.

Consider what you want and what is practical.

The stations and materials as I outline them are suggestions only: there are other ways to get into the work, just as there are many ways to exercise. If another way lends itself to your personality then go with it.

If you are organising a group workout you need to take into consideration the space available to you: ideally each station will have a table for resources and room for people to sit and reflect.

This amount of space may not be available to you so be prepared to be adaptable.

If space is limited then try using the four corners of the room to set out resources—each corner being a 'station' where people can rummage and take what they need.

If resources are limited, suggest that people who are coming might like to bring something with them—offer a *suggestions list* when they book so they have time to find something appropriate.

So, what are these 'Stations'?

It may be helpful to think of 'stations' as being different ways in which you can engage with each of the exercise modules throughout the book. A drawing of a running woman denotes where the exercise section begins in each chapter while the bold initials at the beginning of each individual exercise represents the stations suggested as helpful. These stations are described below with their initials.

SCRIPTURE STATION (SS)

A Bible will, for some people, be an essential resource. Sometimes a particular version can 'hit the spot' but at other times the wording may seem a little obscure; having a couple of different versions available can be helpful to make comparisons. This is not essential, however, and if you have a favourite translation then stick with that.

Soul Workout

At the end of each chapter of the Workout you will be given suggested Scriptures. If you are drawn towards something different then go with that—God may want to draw your attention to something in particular.

I will also suggest different ways you might approach your reading of Scripture. Some of you will be familiar with these methods but they will be new to some and may seem a little scary.

Most of us struggle with new things but don't worry: God is in control and if we are open to his leading he can speak to us whatever method we choose.

Remember that the purpose of a Soul Workout is to become stronger and healthier in God and, through him, in your life. The work at the Scripture station is not to be undertaken as an academic or theological exercise. It is real, not theoretical.

Being alert to 'gut instinct' and feelings is important.

Materials Suggestion List

o   Pen and notebook—usually a journal (see next station)

o   Personal bible: some people prefer to bring their own well-thumbed copy. This has the advantage of familiarity and can be comforting to some people.

o Copies of alternative versions, especially modern versions such as The Message: because the language in these versions is in common usage it can help to clarify or challenge what has previously been unquestioned.

o It can be helpful to provide sheets with bible references: these can be easily carried around and referred to throughout the day. There are too many to suggest here but choose a few Psalms or Gospel stories. Specific suggestions will be made in chapters throughout PART TWO of this book.

JOURNALING STATION (JS)

A notepad and pen are essential items at this station. Many are familiar with journaling and may already use it as a regular feature of their prayer life. The purpose of journaling is to be present to thoughts and feelings that may not be immediately obvious but come as words go down on paper.

Our thoughts are often like gossamer threads—there and then gone before we have really had chance to take them in: journaling allows us to take hold of thoughts and stay with them for a while before moving on.

Writing thoughts down can often crystallise them into something solid instead of seemingly unrelated wispy strands. We are sometimes surprised by the depth of our thoughts and feelings when we journal. We are sometimes amazed when God speaks to us this way—the power of the pen can be great.

There is no formula to journaling. It is a very personal way of communicating—with God and with our own inner being.

Materials Suggestion List

o Obvious—pen and notebook. Although it is usual to suggest people bring these with them, it is always good to have some as a back-up. Biros or pencils can be begged or bought cheaply and notebooks do not have to be expensive. If you are feeling creative and have access to a long stapler then notebooks are easy to make: cut or guillotine a few A4 sheets (try 4) in half to make A5, then fold in half and staple down the middle to make an A6 booklet. If you want to make these look really good then use an outside cover of coloured card! They take minutes to make and only cost a few pence.

o If there is plenty of room on your journaling table then include, if you can, a few poetry books, copies of poems and/or other inspirational books. It is surprising how helpful these can be in personal reflection. They don't have to be overtly spiritual—indeed, some of the most challenging poems may be the ones that seem the least spiritual.

Don't worry if you can't provide these: be practical and don't fret about what you haven't got!

ART STATION (AS)

Art is not universally popular!

It can, however, be an extremely useful tool for anyone doing a workout. Whatever your personal feelings about art, it is worth considering including this station, if at all possible.

Be prepared to hear groaning from some participants—even from those who may have some art experience.

Although I have been painting for a number of years now, I still have a sinking feeling when presented with art materials at workshops or training days: 'What if I make a fool of myself?' 'What if I can't do it?' and, worst of all, 'what if everyone else produces a masterpiece and mine is rubbish?'

Of course, all these fears are unfounded because it's not really about art. It *is* all about being able to explore something of the soul journey in a visual way.

And this is possible for everyone, whether or not they can paint. In fact, it can be harder for artists like me: I have to fight against producing a picture worthy of framing— and that *isn't* what this station is about.

Make it clear to the group that it is not necessary to end up with a 'picture': the aim is to have a dialogue with God about whatever comes to mind during their reflections. They may end up with lines, shapes and/or colours that are only meaningful in the context of their own personal reflections. Working like this can be very revealing and help move someone forward on their soul journey

Materials Suggestion List

- o It is usual when providing art materials to limit them to pastels (oil and/or soft), felt tip pens or coloured pencils.

- o Paint can be messy, so check with the owners of the venue before you commit to providing them. Also remember that if paints are available you will also need to provide water jars, brushes and palettes. Poster paints or acrylics are the usual paints to use. Make sure that people who want to use paints can sit at a table and work.

o Large sheets of paper are good for pastels and paint but can be expensive. If you have old wallpaper stuck in a cupboard then cut it into pieces about A3 size and use the back. Lining paper is cheap to buy and you will only need one roll. Cheap and cheerful!

o Provide kitchen roll and hand wipes: pastels and paints can be messy!

o If you have pencils then don't forget pencil sharpeners and erasers—it may sound obvious but it never ceases to frustrate me how many times I forget these basic things.

o Provide what you can by asking around and getting friends and family to raid their cupboards. Only buy what you need to and buy cheaply: art materials can be prohibitively expensive if you don't shop around.

NATURE STATION (NS)

God is a creator who is in love with His creation. It can be wonderful when we connect with him through nature.

Soul Workout

The ideal for a nature station is to be able to spend some time outside, though this will inevitably be dependent on location and weather.

If the location is suitable and people want to take advantage of the outside then encourage them to do so. The tips on the following page are offered to enable this to be a valuable experience but if the location or weather are not conducive to being outside (or if there are those in the group who don't wish to spend time outside) then having some indoor resources can be a valuable option: look at the materials suggestion list at the end of this chapter. Even where the location suggests a walk or sitting outside, the weather can suddenly change, so having a back-up plan is wise.

Making use of outside space

- Make sure people have a copy of the programme so they know what time to make their way back to the group.

- If the location offers walks outside the venue then offering simple written instructions for a couple of *easy* walks can be very helpful. Remember that in this instance the principal aim is spiritual exercise rather than its physical counterpart.

- Asking people to sign out before going off the premises (and signing back in when they return) is good practice for Health and Safety purposes.

- Offer suggestions for contemplation as outlined in the chapters in PART TWO. Written suggestions offer focus even when people are not physically in the workout environment. Whether walking or sitting, people often like to refresh their memories by referring back to the original prompt.

- The location may offer a garden or other places to sit out. Inform the group at the beginning of the day if there are any restrictions in access to these outside spaces. It is also important to inform them if anyone else will be using the venue and is likely to be taking advantage of the grounds. This will then inform their decision about where to go to get the most from their day.

Materials Suggestion List—Ideas for indoor resources:

o personal photographs of the countryside or the coast;

o any photographs from books and magazines showing the natural world (including animals)—the more varied the better;

Soul Workout

- a basket of raw, fresh vegetables;
- a bowl of fruit;
- a vase of cut flowers;
- an indoor plant;
- pebbles;
- sea-shells;
- a glass of water;
- a small tray or pot of earth.

A few last words about using 'stations' in a workout:

Be practical; use your space wisely; offer participants the best of what you have and don't fret about things you haven't got. Your best offering will be time, space and acceptance of each person's journey.

Part Two

So Now You're Ready To Workout

Using the metaphor to exercise your soul

Chapter 6
In The Changing Room

Arriving at the gym always gives me a sense of satisfaction that I haven't given in to the tempting whisper 'don't go today'. It's a very persuasive little voice and it knows my weak spots. But when I rise to the occasion and refuse to listen, then I find that my motivation levels leap into a different gear: I think, 'Well, now I'm here I might as well work hard and get the most out of it'.

But it wasn't always so.

My mind flits back to an earlier and less happy association with exercise: school games lessons. In particular, I remember the changing rooms with horror and embarrassment and fear stalks my memories. Even though I went to an all-girls school, my dread was acute. In those awkward teenage years, self-consciousness and shyness about the physical changes we were all undergoing meant that getting undressed or dressed in the large communal changing room was akin to purgatory.

But that was only part of it: the practice at the time was that the teacher would stand at the end of the long white-tiled communal shower and watch while all the class ran through. In the early 1960's this practice was considered a normal part of the teacher's job—but there was nowhere to hide and I hated it with a passion.

Bunking off seemed like the only solution. When I could, I hid in the toilets but would sometimes get hauled out of there. When I got a bit older and bolder—and especially when games was timetabled in for the end of the day—I would furtively make my way through the trees bordering the school drive and hop on a bus to town.

I am sure I must have been missed but I don't ever remember being caught out. I hated doing it and only ever bunked-off games—but, needs must: I saw it as defending myself against something too scary to handle.

As you see, my association with changing rooms is not a happy one!

When I first decided to join a gym as an adult, I realised that I would have to face the hurdle of the communal changing room all over again.

In The Changing Room

I well remember my initial reaction when the fitness instructor showed me round: the changing room seemed huge. The showers, curtained for privacy, were at the far end. My mind computed the fact that each shower had a towel hook outside so I would be able to get back to my little bit of changing area without too much embarrassment. But then I would still have to get dried and dressed in close proximity to other women.

The school changing room spectre reared its head and I almost decided not to bother—after all, why was a forty-year old woman putting herself through so much stress?

I signed up.

As time went by I began to relax into the camaraderie of gym changing rooms—though I rarely showered in them (well I'm not *that* brave). Gradually, as my panic subsided, I began to observe the different behaviours of other women I shared the space with. I include these observations because I note that these behaviours are also sometimes evident on Soul Workout days—strange, but true.

Firstly there are The Ditherers. I fitted this category initially. Ditherers haven't finally committed to seeing it through: there is a corner of their mind still saying 'it's not too late. If anyone asks you can say you are not feeling too well—and what's it got to do with anyone else anyway?'

Ditherers often experience a heavy weight in the pit of their stomachs, coupled with the aimless moving of stuff around in their bags as they try to look as if they are getting changed.

They endeavour to melt into the background as they fight anxiety and indecision. They can spend an age in the changing room. They have an internal message that says 'I don't know what to do for the best—shall I go or shall I stay?'

Then there are The Blushers. They may or may not also be Ditherers. Blushers don't want anyone to talk to them because conversation makes them nervous. They know why they're there and it isn't for social networking. They busy themselves in their preparations and are usually to be found in the further corners of the changing room. Their internal message may be, 'Please God, don't let anyone see me.' Blushers who are not ditherers do not stay for long in the changing room for fear of being accosted by a member of the following group:

The Chatterboxes seem to be immune to the body language of either Ditherers or Blushers: they breeze into the room barely drawing breath from conversations outside the door. They head for the busiest part of the room and stake their claim in the centre. Chatterboxes are comfortable with their own bodies and have no embarrassment about walking back from the showers

In The Changing Room

as naked as the day they were born, talking to their neighbours as they go. They are sunny in temperament, laugh a lot and obviously want to make the changing room a happier place—but they can be perceived as a threat or a nuisance by many changing room occupants. I think their internal message is 'Hello everyone. I'm here. Now let's enjoy ourselves.'

The Complainers on the other hand, are never satisfied. As they come into the changing room they are already complaining about everything from the weather to the squeak of the treadmills via the state of the nation. They do all this as they confidently get changed and put all their stuff in a locker. They can still be heard complaining as they go into the gym. The room seems to heave a sigh of relief when they leave. 'Life is against me' is their internal message.

The Lunch Hour Exercisers may equally arrive before or after work. They enter the changing room with intent. They are only interested in exercising—this isn't a social event. Their body language sends a clear message to everyone to stay clear and not try to engage them in conversation—for after all, they only have a limited time. They often strap an ipod to their upper arm to emphasise that they are in a strict 'no-talk' zone. L.H.Es do not linger in the changing room before or after exercise because their internal message is, 'Don't make me late. I'm on a tight schedule.'

Soul Workout

The Workout Fanatics, like L.H.Es, may sport an ipod on the upper arm. They also actively discourage conversation—though the reason for doing so is different: they may not be working to a time limit but they have no social interest in the gym—it is purely a vehicle for exercise. Their sojourn in the changing room is short and often abrupt: their internal message is 'get ready, get out there.'

Last but not least are The Hard Sloggers: these are the ones who, like me, find exercise to be hard work and it would be so easy not to bother. But, we're a stubborn bunch and, having got as far as the changing room, we are determined to get changed and work hard. We can often be heard breathing a sigh of relief when we are getting changed back into our outdoor clothes. We are pleasant to others and will pass the time of day as we get changed. We do not encourage or discourage conversations but prefer not to spend too long in the changing room. Our internal message is 'ok, I'm here, so let's get on with it'.

Although my observations are made with some tongue-in-cheek humour, there is a serious message behind them. Everyone approaches a workout with a great deal of variation in attitude, intention and enthusiasm.

***People who do Soul Workouts** are equally individual in their approach.*

In The Changing Room

The 'changing room', though only part of a metaphor for our purposes, is nonetheless symbolic and needs to be appreciated for the very important job it does.

It may seem an obvious statement but **the changing room provides a physical and psychological boundary** between the outside and the gym itself. It is both a protection from outside distraction and a focus of preparation for work to be done.

Similarly, a ***Soul Workout*** needs protection and focus, otherwise we promise ourselves the time and space and then become distracted and end up wasting the day (or whatever time you have set aside). It is a discipline that offers opportunities to draw close to God and to address personal issues. It also presents similar pressures of time, space, commitment and apprehension to everyone who decides to do it.

Most people have some apprehensions about the workout but that needn't stop the time from being very valuable.

For groups:

People who are part of a group may find it easier to focus, as they have already taken 'time out' to arrive at the venue. Even so, distractions can be all around. *While each person is responsible for finding their own focus, group leaders play an important role in providing the environment in which*

Soul Workout

this focus can be maintained. Having some knowledge about the different behaviours that might be encountered can prove helpful in preserving supportive boundaries.

If you are doing your workout alone, make sure you have cleared the time of demands and obstructions. Lock the door, turn the phone off and refuse to be tempted into looking at your emails. Don't answer the door—or, if you really *have* to, make sure you don't get into any lengthy conversation. If necessary, tell family or friends who may turn up unannounced, that you will be busy that day and absolutely don't get into the 'I'll just do this' scenario.

The changing room of a gym, despite the variety of individuals using it, provides something of a leveller before the work really begins: everyone enters and leaves through the same doors, uses the same facilities and is subject to the same rules.

As a simple exercise to begin, see if you can identify yourself from the list below. If you can say to any of them 'yes, that's me' then spend a minute or two (no longer) asking yourself what causes you to think or behave that way. The likelihood is that you will come face to face to face with your anxieties and

In The Changing Room

apprehensions about what the day will hold for you. At this early time in the workout (remember you are still only in the changing room) all that is required is to acknowledge how you are approaching the day and to commit to being as open to God and yourself as possible. Do not fall into the trap of judging yourself.

If you can't identify with the characters below, don't worry: be yourself and let the workout unfold as it will—but if you sense any feelings of anxiety then try to be specific about what they are.

Anxieties faced squarely can often be found to be less debilitating than unacknowledged anxieties.

- **Ditherers** will struggle to get down to the exercises and will be easily distracted.

If you recognise yourself in this category: use the 'changing room' as a place to consciously decide to take a risk and commit to the process.

- **Blushers** will be tempted to hide in spiritual corners and not get into conversation with God or themselves.

    If you recognise yourself in this category: use the changing room to acknowledge how hard you find it to be vulnerable and ask God to help you enter into conversation with Him.

- **Chatterboxes** will spend the whole time talking to God but not listening. They may be full of joy and spiritual joie de vivre but Soul Workout is a *dialogue*, not a monologue!

    If you recognise yourself in this category: use the changing room to begin the discipline of quietening down, to recognize your need to listen instead of talking and maybe to acknowledge your vulnerability with silence.

- **Complainers** will be set for a miserable day of grumbling at God: at the end of the day they will wonder why they don't feel invigorated or refreshed!

    If you recognise yourself in this category: the changing room needs to be the place where you look for a few 'blessings' to set you up for the day; this may be as simple as appreciating the sun coming through the window or the warmth of the fire on a cold winter's day. Try to find three things that you can thank God for—and then thank him! If you can do this at the beginning of the day it will make a tremendous difference to how you view the rest of your workout.

- **Lunch Hour Exercisers** will be in a rush to get through the workout without taking time to ponder, savour or just 'be'. It is likely that they will have got through 'the work' before lunchtime and then be frustrated that the rest of the day 'is a waste of time'.

If you recognise yourself in this category: try to take time in the changing room to reflect on why you are doing the Workout; depth rather than speed is what you need to be considering. Take time to think about your preferences with regard to Stations and spend a little time considering how you can divide the day up to make maximum use of time. It is important not to fill up every moment with activity—the workout depends on plenty of reflection time when outwardly it may seem that not a lot is happening.

- **A few readers may become Workout Fanatics:** The discipline and format of the workout may appeal to their perceived need to work hard in order to achieve a perfect Christian life. They may be tempted to do the workout every week and to put everything else on one side to do it.

> *If you recognise yourself in this category:* the changing room needs to be a place where you take a look at your reasons and decide if it is truly what you WANT to do. If you recognise any OUGHTs or SHOULDs then use this time to check out what they are all about—you may be surprised with what you find and it may be those things God wants you to bring into the quiet space.

- **Hard Sloggers** will recognise that getting down to the Soul Workout can be difficult but, once committed, will get on with it with a realistic sense of time, space and how to approach it.

  > *If you recognise yourself in this category:* calm your mind; recognise that the time is NOW and be ready to get on with it.

However you approach the workout, and whatever anxieties you hold, remember that this is 'time out' and it is YOUR time. As the door is closed for a time to the ordinary routine of life, you are metaphorically taking off your outer garments and changing into the more suitable clothing of quietness and openness. You are expressing a willingness to let the day unfold without forcing or manipulating any outcome. You are expressing an agreement to spend time with yourself and God and to be proactive in seeking a healthy spiritual life.

In The Changing Room

Going into the changing room is a statement of intent.

For Group Leaders:

Some of you will know the people you are leading and you may already have recognised a few characters; for others, you will be meeting the group for the first time on the day. It is easy (but not very helpful) to be judgemental so it is important to remember that these are *behaviours* we are concerned with—and a behaviour does not make a person. Using these characterisations is a way of recognising and confronting fears and apprehensions that may be around within the group as the day starts.

You might want to flag them up for the group so that each individual can consider how they come to the day and what, if any, their particular anxieties are. This is one reason why keeping safe boundaries is important: no-one should feel judged or ridiculed but be allowed (as with everything else in the workout) to use what is helpful and discard the rest.

Safe boundaries include allowing someone to sit in a corner if they choose or asking people not to engage others in conversation during the exercises. Safe boundaries also include explaining how the programme is set out so that participants are not left wondering about the unknown or becoming anxious about being pressurised into sharing anything personal.

Your role as Group Leader is to make the day as valuable as possible for each participant. Providing an accepting environment for each person is not always easy—some are so timid it is hard to know whether they are 'connecting' with the metaphor while others seem to want to question the metaphor (and everything else) so much, you wonder if they are procrastinating for any particular reason.

Be sensitive to each person but stick with your programme or you may find that some of the characteristic behaviours I have outlined above hijack the workout at the outset.

Chapter 7
Don't Neglect Your Warm Up

At this point you are prepared for your workout; you have arrived at the venue and have settled yourself within the group—or, if doing the workout alone at home, you have closed the door, turned the phone off and sent a message to everyone that you are unavailable. Wherever you are doing the workout you are only available to yourself and God.

All well and good—but you are not *quite* ready yet to go in deep and meaningfully: if you try to, you may unconsciously sabotage your day.

We need to go back to our metaphor to understand how important the Warm Up is:

Trying to work out without warming up is asking for trouble. Muscles need to be stretched and literally 'warmed up' to prevent injury. If you skip warm up and dive straight into serious exercise you run the risk

Soul Workout

of ending up with visits to the physiotherapist instead of visits to the gym. Muscles will become strained, ligaments may become torn and you will be in pain.

When I first began going to the gym I felt silly doing warm ups: stretching arms and legs with a series of floor exercises seemed like a waste of time. Now I'd made the effort to get there I wanted to get on with it: I had my exercise programme worked out by a Fitness Instructor and it was tempting to begin with the iconic bike or treadmill—after all, that's what you expect to be doing in a gym!

But the instructor had done her job well and she impressed on me the benefits of this initial stage. At the start of every workout I would stretch each muscle group, coaxing my muscles into life in a gentle, controlled way.

It helped my body take the much greater demands I would shortly make on it.

Inevitably there came a time when I was in a bit of a rush so didn't bother with either the warm up or the cool down—I dived straight into my ten minutes on the bike, followed by the rest of my programme.

I lived to regret it: aching muscles, soreness on moving and more twinges than I had been used to. I quickly went back to my routine.

Don't Neglect Your Warm Up

To change the metaphor for a minute, doing a warm up is like gently accelerating away from the kerb instead of letting your foot floor the accelerator as soon as the brake is off: the latter is a move both dangerous and damaging.

So, my first foray into a gym gave me a set routine for warming up and, naively, I thought that it was the only way to do it. Over the years I have learnt to use different stretching exercises as a way of loosening up and freeing my muscles to take on something more challenging. But I still revert to the original exercises from time to time.

In other words, I don't need to be rigid about *how* I warm up but do need to be mindful of *why* I do it—and then I need to make sure I *DO* it.

What is so important about warming up for a Soul Workout?

The problem about missing your warm up is that you are likely to be distracted, fidgety or be unable to find your 'still point' for reflective meditation. It is as if you are trying to get maximum use out of stiff and cold spiritual muscles.

It usually takes a little bit of gentle coaxing to quieten ourselves down and enter a space that is both intimate and sacred. There is a danger that a part of the mind will dwell on the past and part will fast forward to the future.

Soul Workout

Something is needed to bring us into the power of the present moment. The warm up does just that.

For instance, I may have prepared myself as we described in the last chapter but a remnant of my mind may still be registering annoyance with the junk mail that arrived in the post this morning. As I work at trying to put this feeling out of my mind, another part of my brain may be anticipating how I want this special day to go and working out how best to achieve it.

I put myself into difficulties if I try to go into a workout with such distractions and agendas on my mind.

The answer to this dilemma is to spend a few minutes deliberately and consciously bringing myself into a state of being truly *IN* the present moment. This is what a Soul Workout warm-up is about.

SUGGESTIONS FOR YOUR WARM UP ROUTINE

Spend a total of about 20 minutes on these exercises.

The warm-up needs to contain the two set elements of the **Stilling** and **Reflective** exercises outlined below but may also include an **optional physical** element to begin with.

The optional element is for those who *want, and are able*, to prepare with a set of very gentle physical exercises. If you decide to do them then the beginning of the warm up is when they are most effective.

First of all, stand up with your arms down by your side and your feet placed slightly apart. Look straight ahead. Now imagine that an invisible cord has come down from above and attached itself to the top of your head. This cord gently draws you up to your full height so that you are standing tall while keeping both feet firmly on the ground. Gently move your head up and down, as if being moved by the cord, until it feels comfortably straight—it helps to focus on something at eye level. You should be feeling straight but relaxed. Notice how your spine stretches without putting undue pressure on it. Stay in this position for a few seconds.

- Move from this first position by bringing your arms up from your side in a slow sweep until they are straight above your head and stretch your hands upwards, as if trying to reach something just out of grasp. Look straight ahead of you as you do this in order to maintain balance. Now, stretch up on tiptoe by raising your heels slowly off the floor. Hold this position for a second or two, before slowly lowering your heels and bringing your arms back in a gentle sweep to your sides. Keep looking straight ahead as you do this. Repeat three or four times.

- Continue standing with your feet slightly apart, bring your arms round to the front so they are straight and level with your chest. Clasp your hands together and gently push against each other: feel the tension going up your arms. Hold for a few seconds. Relax and let go. Now take your arms to the back. Grasp your hands together and push them gently away from you: don't force your arms away from your body: just a little pressure is sufficient. Hold for a second or two before letting go and letting your arms relax by your side. Remain standing.

- Sometimes facial muscles need to be stretched— we have many facial muscles and they are all capable of feeling tension. Bring your face into an exaggerated scowl by furrowing your brow, pressing your lips together and screwing your eyes up (it doesn't matter what you look like— even if you are doing this as a group, you are all in it together!). From there, stretch your face wide: open your mouth and give a wide smile, open your eyes wide and feel your forehead stretch out and up. Let your face return to its normal expression.

- Relax by gently shaking out your hands and feet as if you are shaking drops of water off.

Whether or not you have done the optional element, you are now ready to move into the two set essentials to your warm up routine:

Stilling:

o Sit comfortably: you may need to shuffle around a bit to find optimum comfort but, as you do, be aware of your body sitting in the chair or on the floor. Be aware of the chair or the floor holding you and of the physical space that is 'you'.

o Close your eyes and become aware of any external sounds. It may be the sound of distant traffic, a clock ticking or an odd creak and groan from the radiator. Hear it but don't strain to listen to it: by acknowledging its presence as a fact you are less likely to be distracted by it.

o Moving inward, become aware of any *internal* noise. You may be aware of your heartbeat, the sounds of your stomach or noises in your ears. You may hear yourself breathing. You may also become aware of your noisy head! Our thoughts are shaped as words and we often *hear* ourselves thinking. Without judgement or criticism, hear these thoughts but don't strain to listen to them. Accept them into your space without giving them centre stage: they are just a part of you.

o Now consciously become aware of *how* you are breathing: when we are tense or anxious our breathing is shallow and fast. It comes from high up in our chests. When we are relaxed, our breath originates from lower down in the diaphragm and is slower. Try taking a deep slow breath in from this lower place. When you have taken in as much as is comfortable, hold it for a second or two before slowly breathing out. Try this deep breathing a few times before letting your breathing return to a normal level.

o *Some of you may be used to breathing exercises such as this through Yoga or other fitness or relaxation regimes so as an extension of this exercise you might like to try the following:*

As you breathe in, try imagining you are taking in the simple, fresh, pure love of God. As you breathe out imagine you are letting go of the stale, unhealthy, complicated tangle of life. Don't try to analyse any of this but merely see it as breathing in life and breathing out the waste products.

o Another way of doing this is to have a mantra: you might try breathing in to YAH and out to WEH (Yahweh is the Jewish word for God) *or* breathe in to JE and out to SUS (Jesus). Spend a few minutes on this way of stilling yourself.

***Before you begin the second part of the warm up** spend few minutes in silence and imagine that deep within yourself you have a 'Still Point'—a place where there is no thought, no time and where you don't have to do or plan anything. It is a place of 'being': a place of stillness and peacefulness. This does take practice and you may not be able to get there but, whether you can or can't, it is worth sitting with the silence.*

Reflective Exercise

Only use one of these exercises for your warm up routine: there will be other opportunities to use them throughout the day:

- Use some quiet reflective music (have the volume at a comfortable level so that it is more than just background music but doesn't blast you out). Begin to consciously focus on what you can hear. Spend a few minutes letting the sound wash over you and into you.

Even if it is a familiar piece of music, you may be surprised to hear new notes or instruments you have never noticed before. Allow yourself to be taken into it and, in so doing, see it as carrying you into the intimate and sacred place where you can begin to connect with your spiritual self.

- Using photographs, prints or paintings is a good way of getting into a reflective space. Spend a few minutes settling yourself down with the picture of your choice and begin by taking in the whole of it for a few minutes. What is the picture about? How does it make you feel? Don't have any pre-conceived ideas about where your thoughts should be directed but be aware of what your chosen picture is suggesting. Allow your emotions to be engaged if you feel drawn that way but don't try to force anything.

Now focus in on one aspect of the picture: what drew you to that particular detail? Does it have anything to say to you about your feelings as you enter your sacred space? Does it form connections for you in terms of how you see yourself at this point? Make no judgements or criticisms but use any awareness as stepping stones into a very special internal place. This is the place from which your workout can begin.

- If you are a tactile person, you might like to use a variety of items as visual aids: things like pebbles, flower petals (real or artificial), leaves, pine cones, twigs, feathers, a bowl of water and towel, ribbons of various colours, a variety of differently textured textiles are just some suggestions.

  To get the most out of your items you need to use your senses: touch them, stroke them, look at each detail, smell them, listen to any noise they might make when you move them through your hands or drop them on to the floor/table. I don't recommend trying to taste them unless they are edible!

  Be aware of how each item makes you feel. What does each item remind you of? Where is your sense of the sacred in these items?

  By reflecting on them in this manner you are allowing them to draw you into an internal space where you can begin to reflect on who you are in relation to the physical world around you. It can also help you to make connections between the physical and spiritual worlds you inhabit.

- Light a candle and sit quietly. Focus on the light. This very simple exercise can be a very effective way of moving from the external to the internal.

Soul Workout

> Allow your thoughts to roam freely but be aware of where your thoughts go and whether there is any pattern to your reflections. Stay with this for a few minutes, then begin to focus your thoughts on the space you are in being intimate and sacred—a place where you can be completely yourself. Make no judgement. Accept yourself *as you are* in the external and internal places you inhabit.

The Warm Up is now complete and you are now ready to move into the deeper exercises of the Soul Workout. Hopefully, you have moved into a place where you can begin to flex those spiritual muscles without giving yourself an injury.

For Group Leaders:

It will be part of your role to 'set the scene' for the rest of the workout by providing the warm-up exercise. Leading a group involves being sensitive as well as prepared so, unless you know the group well and know that the optional element of a physical warm-up would be appropriate, it is best to leave it out and concentrate on the Stilling and Reflection exercises.

The group will need you to talk them through the Stilling Exercise so familiarise yourself with the format before the day: try writing it out beforehand—use your own words if you prefer so that it feels more natural to you—and practice reading it aloud. Then on the day you will be able to lead the group proficiently and smoothly.

Using music to take you into the Reflective Exercise: using an *un*familiar piece of music helps people listen more closely. However, of more importance, is that the music is quietly reflective, at a comfortable listening level and offers an opportunity for individuals to move into their personal soul work. Keep to instrumentals unconnected with lyrics or associated with popular advertising as these might prove distracting.

Using images or tactile items requires you to be imaginative and prepared. Supply enough for everyone to have a choice but keep things simple. Decide on what you will use beforehand and stick with that.

The group should be still, quiet and ready for the rest of the workout by the end of the warm-up. You may also notice a subtle feeling of being a part of a community emerging—albeit temporary. Enjoy leading them!

Chapter 8
Cardiovascular Work

Aerobic (another name for cardiovascular) exercise is sure to make your heart beat faster and bring you out in a sweat! But, don't let that put you off: it's designed to keep you healthy.

A healthy body is one where the heart is capable of pumping oxygen around in the blood without undue stress and where the veins and arteries are well maintained to allow free circulation.

The word **'aerobic'** means 'with oxygen': aerobic exercise aims at improving our oxygen intake, which, in turn, makes our bodies work more efficiently and energetically. Without oxygen we die. The term **'cardio'** (heart) **'vascular'** (circulation) relates to the organ and channels through which this life-giving movement can take place.

Cardiovascular Work

Though these two terms are interchangeable I will use 'cardiovascular' as it describes more satisfactorily what I want to convey in terms of the Soul Workout.

Cardiovascular exercise can take many forms but whatever its structure it will require us to make repetitive and rhythmic movements regularly at a moderately intense pace. The most familiar pieces of cardiovascular equipment in a gym are the treadmill, bike, rower and stepper. So, for the purpose of our metaphor, we will stick with these.

My experiences with treadmills are many and varied. There was the small manual treadmill we bought for use at home: it was so difficult to get the rollers to move that I was out of puff and sweaty just trying to start the thing off. There was no question of getting a decent rhythm going as my muscles were shot before a minute was out. It didn't last long.

Then there was the treadmill at my first gym. I was completely out of my comfort zone at that point. I kept forgetting how to start, stop and change speeds on the different pieces of equipment in my programme. (My family would tell you that I don't 'do' technology: I'm not even fully conversant with the TV remote control.)

Soul Workout

The instructors were very patient but weren't always free to deal with this totally incompetent woman—and I felt that I had exhausted the goodwill of other gym users on that particular morning. I managed to start the treadmill up but got momentarily distracted as I hit the 'increase speed' button: my finger stayed down on the button a fraction longer than intended. A second or two elapsed without undue problem but then the machine registered that *this* health-nut *really* wanted to work out. It obliged!

Suddenly I was running and hanging on for dear life to the bar at the front that monitors heart rate. I have no idea what this was recording but my heart was certainly working overtime as I fought to remember how to reduce speed quickly. I hit the 'emergency stop' bar and nearly catapulted across the gym. Why had it taken seconds to speed up but stopped dead immediately?

The fitness instructor came running over to see if I was okay. My fellow gym-mates were solicitous. I was deeply embarrassed. Needless to say, I have never made that mistake again. Now I am careful to take my speed up in steady increments and have learnt to slow down in the same way. The 'emergency stop' bar is a thing to fear.

My association with bikes is not as dramatic but has had its funny side over the years.

Cardiovascular Work

I am, not to put too fine a point on it, a little on the small side. At four feet ten inches tall, there is not much in life that comes 'made to measure'. From supermarket shelves to bus seats my height puts me at a disadvantage: I stretch or dangle accordingly. There is nothing for it but to get on with life.

Exercise bikes can prove a little tricky.

We owned one that lived in the bedroom for some time. I was all for getting it—but had not considered the logistics of seat and pedal position versus height. The bike conspired against me. Even in its lowest seating position, I could not reach the pedals comfortably enough to rotate them without doing myself an injury.

The bike became a clotheshorse for a few years before we gave it away.

Gym bikes are a little less daunting but I still have to have them on the lowest possible setting. At the gym I go to now I have to use a bike with a back (as opposed to the upright ones with no back) and, even then, I have to get a cushion from a chair near reception and wedge myself a little further forward so that I can pedal comfortably. I've no idea what my fellow gym-users think about a woman who has to work out with aid of a cushion.

As for rowing machines: I have studiously avoided them and will continue to do so.

Finally, to complete this little tour around some of the cardiovascular equipment to be found in most gyms, we come to the 'stepper'. This piece of equipment may have different names and come in a variety of guises but its aim is the same: for me it is an instrument of torture. In the past my gym programme has said 'stepper: 5 minutes' or 'stepper: maximum 10 minutes'.

Well, I've got news for gym instructors: this out-of-condition woman in the later stages of middle age can only manage a minute without coming out in a sweat and two minutes without feeling that her legs are about to drop off. Steppers, in whatever shape they come, are for those who are determined to work hard and can cope with heat and perspiration.

But I persevere.

The thing about cardiovascular exercise is that it makes you work at the really important things: without a healthy heart and efficient oxygen-transporting system our bodies begin to go into a decline. We become easily fatigued, less able to fight off infections and become altogether more sluggish and lethargic. Getting a sweat on is good for you.

Cardiovascular Work

But of course it depends on how much of a sweat: there is a vast difference between working hard enough to be hot and a little out of breath and being so breathless you can't talk and so hot you feel faint. Working too hard can be as unhealthy as not putting an effort in at all. It all depends on degree.

Transposing the metaphor into our Soul Workout, we can see that our relationship with God is at the **heart** of the Christian faith. How that relationship powers and enables movement in the rest of our lives is the equivalent of the oxygen-transporting **vascular** system.

Developing and maintaining our God-relationship takes time and energy. Most of us accept the need to put effort into our faith journeys to prevent spiritual debilitation but can we try *too* hard?

I believe we can. Just as with its physical equivalent, too much effort on our part can, in my opinion, be spiritually damaging.

'Surely not,' I can hear some of you saying, 'you can never put too much into your relationship with God.' But, beware the heat and sweat of too much struggle: if God's love is a gift then there is no way we can earn it through hard work; to try to do so could mean that we miss what God wants for us. This is why Soul

Soul Workout

Workout gives space for silence, self-awareness, reflection, observation and an awareness of the Mystery of God.

As with any relationship, our God-relationship is two-way. I am very sure that God puts more in than we do to make our relationship work but we need to do our bit without trying to take over from God. What do I mean?

Remember my mishap with the runaway treadmill? There was nothing wrong with the treadmill itself; it was working as it was supposed to work. It was my ignorance and anxiety that caused the problem. By trying too hard to do the right thing I ended up doing the *wrong* thing and nearly caused myself an injury.

Here's an example of what it means to work too hard spiritually:

Jane loved God and she wanted to do his will. She felt sure he had a Ministry for her. If only she knew what it was he wanted her to do! She fasted, she prayed, she read her scriptures. She laid fleeces (see the story of Gideon in Judges chapter 6) and she attended every meeting she could where there might be a 'word from the Lord'. All to no avail.

She was persuaded one way and then another by this person and that book. Her family began to complain that she was never at home and her boss told her to focus or she might find herself out of a job.

Jane became *dis*-spirited. She reckoned that she must have gone wrong somewhere and that God couldn't love her because she was a bad person.

She tried harder. She bought Bible commentaries so that she could better understand the scriptures. She fasted for two days at a time instead of one and her prayers became lengthy confessions of all her perceived sins, alongside prolonged pleas for forgiveness.

God remained silent.

She was sure now that she must be too bad to be loved.

She became depressed.

Her husband couldn't cope and, after a long time of trying to reason with her, he left. Jane blamed herself but, deep down, she blamed God: after all, she had only wanted to please him and do his work—and look how he had repaid her.

'But' she reasoned, 'a God of love wouldn't be like that, so the only explanations are that God is either not a loving God or he doesn't exist at all. Whichever one is

Soul Workout

true,' she thought, 'I have lost everything because of believing a lie.'

Now Jane became aggressively anti-Christian and disassociated herself from all her Christian friends. Now she would only believe and trust in herself.

This completely fictitious tale is extreme but could easily be true. It is a composite of many true stories I have encountered, both in counselling and Spiritual Direction. It shows how debilitating it can be to try too hard. In the end it becomes less about Jane's relationship with God and more about becoming self-absorbed and self-reliant. Jane stopped trusting in anyone other than herself.

I think Jane was missing what God was actually saying to her: as with all of us, he says 'I love you as you are. Be yourself.' If she had taken time to hear this, she may have understood that her 'ministry' was to care for the people around her and to be fully engaged with her life in the present. She would have understood that God speaks as much through the sight of the first snowdrop or a smile from a stranger as through a word of scripture or prophecy. God speaks to us in many different ways but most of these ways are very understated and easily missed if we are waiting to be zapped by miracle and 'enlightenment'.

Cardiovascular Work

The trap that Jane fell into was that she felt the onus was on *her* to discover what God wanted. The more she tried to decipher the mystical code she assumed was hiding the truth from her, the more she felt out of control. She then began to fear she wasn't good enough: after all, if she couldn't decode the cipher, how would she be able to do the work?

It was then only a short journey to seeing herself as unlovable; it became easy to convince herself that she was a bad person and from there it was easy to blame God for doing this to her; the next logical step was to turn her back on God and faith.

All this because she was trying too hard.

If only she could have seen that God would not put smoke-screens up to confuse her: If she had stopped and listened to the 'still small voice' in her soul instead of drowning it out by working harder and harder, then she would have understood what God wanted for her. If she could have read scripture as a love story between God and us (including herself), that being 'in the moment' with God in silent prayer can be more meaningful than endless entreaty, she would have been able to see through the sweat and toil. As for fasting: well, there may have been times God wanted her to fast for specific reasons but she had used it as a ritual aimed at making him

Soul Workout

listen to her—and it backfired because God will not be manipulated by us.

Jane had made her spiritual journey such hard work that it wiped her out.

So, how can we get a spiritual sweat on without giving ourselves a heart attack?

The most important aspect of this kind of spiritual exercise is to be open to God's surprises. We often have expectations of how God will reveal himself or what he wants us to focus on but sometimes he can take us by surprise—if we let him.

SUGGESTED CARDIOVASCULAR EXERCISES

The exercises offered below may be familiar or totally new. Ask, 'what am I attracted to?' rather than 'what am I comfortable with?' and go with the attraction. God may want you out of your comfort zone. He may want to show you new ways to pray or bring new understanding: you may notice a new emphasis or word in a familiar scripture or see your faith in a different light.

Cardiovascular Work

All the 'Stations' will suggest ways of allowing yourself to 'be' with God as you are. Don't try too hard: if you feel you are beginning to struggle then put down the exercise and ask yourself what is making you feel like that. Use the following acronym:

S—stay with your feelings but let go of the exercise

T—*think about other times when you felt this way: what you were doing at the time?

O—*open yourself up to what God might be saying in the present about your past.

P—*pray that God will heal what needs to be healed for you to be closer to Him.

***Remember** that this may overlap with situations to be covered in the weight-resistance work. If so, acknowledge this but focus now on how it impacts on your relationship with God. You can return to other aspects later: remember the importance of working on the heart and life-blood of your faith before tackling anything else.*

A REMINDER

Each of the exercises will be identified with initials depicting the relevant 'station': where more than one set of initials is listed it means the exercise can

Soul Workout

be approached in different ways—decide which is appropriate.

Exercises are divided into Basic and Advanced to take different levels of experience into account.

Decide which ONE exercise you feel drawn to: every exercise offers a prayerful encounter with God. Your intuition is invaluable here so *go with what feels right to you at that moment.* Use the exercise suggestions as you wish but don't forget that God may want to surprise you!

BASIC CARDIOVASCULAR EXERCISES

a)   **SS**

Read *ONE* of the following Bible passages:

Matthew 4 v 18-22: Calling of the Disciples

John 4 v 4-26: The woman at the well

Luke 15 v 11-24: Prodigal Son

Luke 8 v 22-25: Jesus calms the storm

- ❖ When you have chosen a passage read it through slowly. This way of prayerfully reading scripture is called ***Lectio Divina.***

Cardiovascular Work

- ❖ You may want to stay with one word, phrase or section from the passage—*or* you might want to take it as a whole. Do whatever you feel drawn to.

- ❖ Re-read the passage & then spend some time meditating on what it is saying to you.

- ❖ You might find it helpful to use the following guidelines in your meditations:—

What does this passage seem to be saying / teaching me? What does it tell me about Jesus / God?

How do I feel about what it is showing me? What do I want to say to God from these reflections?

Have I any sense of him replying? How does this feel? Have I any sense of movement in my relationship with God?

b) SS; JS

Read a psalm (Psalms 23, 100, 121 may be good ones to try—but only choose one) and then try rewriting it in your own words—maybe relating it to life as it is now. Where appropriate, try making the words more personal by writing in your own name. Once you have finished writing, spend time

Soul Workout

reading and reflecting on your chosen passage: talk to God about how it feels to make this passage personal.

c) **JS**

'Dear God, I am writing this letter to you because . . .'

Now *write the letter*: remember that it is between you and God alone. The aim of it is to express where you feel you are in your God-relationship at this moment. Take your time and be completely honest—if you feel you are struggling or even if you feel you don't have a relationship to speak of then, say so. Equally, if you feel very close to God at this moment then express that—maybe as a love letter.

d) **SS; AS**

Begin by reading one of the following passages:

Luke 8 v 22-25 (Jesus calms the storm) *OR* Psalm 23

Spend a little time reflecting on the passage—what you understand by it, how it makes you feel, and go with any thoughts that present themselves about what you have been reading. When ready, begin to use these reflections as a focus to express yourself through art. Remember that this is not about turning out a masterpiece but about letting God speak to you through marks, shapes, colours, textures. If you are not sure how to start, then try closing your eyes and make some marks on the page with your non-dominant hand. Open your eyes and spend a few minutes looking at these marks. Do they suggest anything? Does a shape vaguely resemble something? Try putting some colour on or redefining a shape—allow it to develop as it will. As you work, talk to God about whatever comes to mind and listen for him speaking to you about whatever he wants! Free yourself from the need to 'produce' something but rather spend the time in a creative dialogue with God. At the end of your time you may find that you've completely moved away from the scripture meditation—but that's okay.

e) **NS**

(Dependant on weather & location) take a slow stroll outside. *Allow your senses to take in the natural world around you.* Stop to listen to any noise but listen also to the silence. Take both sound and silence into your reflections.

Take time to observe whatever is in front of you— if you see something from the corner of your eye then turn to face it, observe it as fully as you can.

Reach out and touch a variety of objects, noting the different textures; recognise your likes and dislikes in these varieties. Be aware of the different smells of nature—some delicate and subtle, some overpowering and 'in your face'; some sweet and pleasant, some pungent and disagreeable. It may not be possible to 'taste' anything from your stroll but imagine, if you can, the taste of seasonal fruit—or your favourite fruit. Spend a few minutes savouring either real or imagined taste. During your stroll be mindful of the God who created such diversity and such beauty. Take time to thank him for his created world. Use whatever language comes naturally to you to quietly praise him for his bounty.

On your return you may want to continue reflecting on your stroll. In particular, use this further time to 'be' as a created person in God's world. How does this speak of your relationship with your creator?

f) NS: AS: JS

If the weather is inclement, the location not conducive or if you don't want to leave the premises then you might like to do the following visualisation to see how and where it connects for you:

Sit quietly with your eyes closed and relax. Imagine that you can see a tree in front of you and take a minute or two to take a look around it, taking note of how tall and broad it is and what season you are viewing your tree in—are its branches bare? Are there new leaves or blossom appearing? Is it in full leaf or is its foliage turning golden with Autumn?

Now imagine that you can see the roots going into the earth: are the roots deep and soaking up nourishment or does it seem as if they are shallow and struggling to anchor and provide adequate stability?

Now consider the bark surrounding the trunk of the tree: do you get a sense of whether it is thick and gnarled with the years or is it thin, fragile and flaking off in places?

Move up in your imagination to see the branches: do they reach upwards with a sense of strength and energy or do they bend over towards the ground, as if the weight of the foliage is too great? What foliage can you see?

Take note of how this tree makes you feel. Don't try to make it anything other than it is.

Now for the second part of the visualisation:

If you can, *try to see yourself as the tree* and imagine that each section—roots, bark, branches and foliage—is telling you something about your spiritual journey. What do you learn from it? What might God be saying to you through these images?

From these reflections try writing or drawing what you see and feel—let God continue to open your soul through these channels.

Let your imagination loose in this exercise and try to by-pass your logic.

ADVANCED CARDIOVASCULAR EXERCISES

a)   SS; JS; AS

Read *ONE* of the following Bible passages:

Matthew 4 v 18-22: Calling of the Disciples

John 4 v 4-26: The woman at the well

Luke 15 v 11-24: Prodigal Son

Luke 8 v 22-25: Jesus calms the storm

Re-read your chosen passage and begin to imagine yourself in the scene. Now with your eyes closed, go through the story slowly in your imagination, as if you are actually there: take notice of who

Cardiovascular Work

you are in the story; what is happening; how you are feeling; what you might say to Jesus; what he might say to you. Be aware of sights, sounds, smell, the feel of things around you; let your imagination loose and use your senses to get into the story.

Once you have let the story slowly unfold in your imagination you might want to journal it—writing often helps to further the experience for you. Record not only what happened *but how you felt*.

Or, if you prefer visual images, try drawing something of your journey through the story—use colour, shapes, marks, to express yourself. Hold a dialogue with God as you do this: it will deepen your sense of relationship with God. Once you have developed this reflection in either written or drawn form, *spend a few minutes reviewing how you feel about the process you have gone through*: how were you feeling before you started the exercise? Has this changed? If so, how are you feeling now?

What has made the difference? Has anything in particular drawn you closer to God during the exercise? You might like to record this review in your journal.

Soul Workout

b) SS; JS

Write your own prayer: (you might like to base it on one of the great prayers in the Bible. Suggestions for reading are:

Luke 1 v 46-55 (Magnificat) or Psalm 8

Remember: cardiovascular exercise is all about your relationship with God, so don't use this time as a written list of people or situations to bring to prayer! Use it as a way of speaking to God about where you are with him: if you are full of love—then express it; if you are full of remorse or guilt—then tell him (knowing that confession is followed by forgiveness); if you have a lot to thank him for—then do it. Prayer is not a formula but a conversation with God. Write ***and*** listen. Be honest and reach down into the depths of your soul to express what needs to be expressed: writing the prayer is of secondary importance—of primary importance is to *pray* it in your soul!

c) SS; JS; NS; AS

God, Jesus, Creation and Me: Go out for a walk if possible or, if not, use pictures or items from the Nature station to inform your reflections. Be observant and alert to all that you are taking in: if you are outside be aware of temperature and light as well as what is around; if you are inside and can look out, observe what you can of the outside space.

As you walk or sit, consider the **vastness** of creation, the **detail** to be found in the smallest things and the huge **variety** of colour and form to be found in the world.

Use these words (*vastness, detail* and *variety)* in your mind and observe not just what you see but how you **feel** about what you see.

If you are outside you might like to bring something back from your walk to remind you of these reflections or perhaps you would like to sketch something that catches your eye while you are out.

Whether outside or in, journal your observations

You are now ready for the next part of this exercise:

Read JOHN 1 v 1-5. It is time to put your observations and reflections together with the reading—and see where it takes you. The Mystery of creation is beyond our understanding but be open to anything that God might want to reveal to you.

Soul Workout

Now is the time to dig deeply into your soul for you are also a created being. How does the possibility of being in relationship with this Creator God and this Jesus who is the Word of God, sit with you?

Can you recognise it as a reality in your life? If not, do you want to?

Can you ask (and trust) God to break through any barriers of relationship?

Be honest about any struggles you are having as you do this exercise—it is no easy thing to contemplate creation and relationship together.

For Group Leaders:

In order to get the most out of this part of the workout the participants need you to explain the metaphor so that they can link it to the exercises.

As you open the metaphor to them use whatever will be helpful from this chapter but make it your own: let your personality shine out and set the scene in a way that feels as comfortable as possible. It is important that you explain any jargon e.g. 'cardiovascular' will need an explanation: as a tutor once said to me 'don't commit assumicide'—in other words, don't assume people know what you mean without explanation. But keep such explanations short and simple.

Once the metaphor has been opened up it is time for people get on with the day themselves. However you have set out the space and whichever stations you are using, provide appropriate handouts containing the exercises: the ones above are suggestions only so don't be restricted by them.

You may want to include a short opening paragraph on the handouts to remind people of the metaphor and how it relates to a soul workout *or* you might want to have a flip chart in a strategic place in the room with a short reminder. Whatever you choose to do on this, it is now time to trust that the metaphor works.

If you have given everyone a run-down of the programme then people will know what time to make their way back—lunch time usually signals the end of this period on a full day.

Chapter 9
Weight Resistance

Have you noticed that sometimes life has a way of making us feel weak and bowed down? We say things like 'I can't cope any more', 'when will it end?' 'I want it to stop' or 'I feel like I'm going to blow'.

There are times in life when we feel as if we are living inside a pressure cooker.

This chapter is about learning to carry whatever life is weighing us down with and do it without injuring ourselves. Notice I don't say that it will teach you how to *get rid* of the burdens of life or offer techniques to live a stress-*free* existence: it just can't be done.

Even with God in your life you have to face the reality of living in an imperfect world amongst imperfect people—and, hey, that includes me and you!

What a Soul Workout offers is a chance to readjust the load so that we carry it more effectively until we can put it down. Sometimes, but not always, we are able to have a bit of a rest before picking up another life-burden. There are occasions when we have to carry several life-burdens at the same time. Soul Workout aims to help us do it without collapsing under the weight.

This chapter will look at those burdens we carry because we have to; those we carry because we choose to and those we carry because we are unable to say 'no'. We will explore how to reassess our personal life-burdens in the light of our relationship with God.

We must return to our metaphor: In a gym the weight resistance exercises are designed to help us build strong bone and muscle so that our bodies can bear the day-to-day strains of life. Strength is built by gradually increasing the weight we are exposed to so that over a period of time the body can withstand more pressure: this is done either by working directly with weights that are lifted, or by 'resistance' machines which make us push against the action of the machine, in order to 'resist' the weight and so strengthen our core muscles.

If anyone tries to start at a weight level that is too high for them the result is pain, strain and, maybe, long-term injury. You need to start low and build up slowly: each increment being difficult for a time until your body becomes used to the weight.

Weight resistance is not easy. It takes time, staying power and stamina.

I have a love-hate relationship with weight-resistance machines. There have been those where I felt I was doing okay and making slow but satisfying progress. There have been machines that have done me no favours at all. Knowing where to call a halt is an essential piece of wisdom. These days I concentrate on cardiovascular work so I generally give the resistance machines a wide berth: my excuse is that I already work with weights on a daily basis—and that's just carrying my handbag around!

Seriously, I have had my ups and downs with this type of exercise. Being stubborn, I have occasionally tried to work too hard on the machines; the consequence has been to put too much pressure on parts of my body that are already struggling—especially my knees. Several courses of physiotherapy have taught me that sometimes saying 'no' and finding other, gentler ways to keep muscles fit is necessary. We will return to this aspect of our metaphor in more depth later.

For now, let me say that weight-resistance work can find muscles where you never knew you had them. It is usual to work muscle *groups* rather than individual muscles

Weight Resistance

and a workout targets all the main muscle groups in your body. Some weight exercises target calf muscles while others work on thighs; arms and shoulders are worked differently to chest and stomach muscles. Lifting dumb-bells requires a certain kind of posture while some weight-resistance machines require you to stand or sit in different positions. You adopt the wrong pose at your peril for then your muscles are vulnerable.

When you work in harmony with weights and machine you soon begin to feel the benefits of toned muscles, strong bones, an energised body and a sense of wellbeing.

How weight-resistance works outside the gym.

Ordinary everyday things can every so often make us flip! Sometimes relatively small matters weigh heavily on us.

Human relationships, work, finance, health, leisure-time (or lack of it) and, for some, church, are the nitty-gritty of our daily existence. They take up the majority of our time and energy. They can sap us. They require regular maintenance and strengthening. We ignore such maintenance at our peril.

It only needs a crisis in one of these areas for us to feel we are going over the edge. A crisis in one or more areas may become a disaster from which we struggle to recover.

Having a faith and being spiritually aware does not make us immune from catastrophes but it can make all the difference in how we deal with them and, ultimately, how we come through them.

Come with me to the imaginary homes of two women, Penny and Kate, whose families are both going through difficult times. Both women come from similar backgrounds and both are in their forties. Furthermore, they both juggle jobs and home.

They may live similar lives on the outside but their inner struggles are very different.

Penny is feeling very insecure at the moment: her job as Senior Sales Assistant in a large retail unit is in jeopardy, following a successful take-over by a rival company. Tensions are running high as a new manager has been appointed. It is common knowledge that he has a remit to prune costs by reducing staffing levels. Penny can't afford to lose her job: she is a single mum with a mortgage and has no-one else to help her financially.

Furthermore, Penny is dealing with tensions in her personal life: her mother, who she is very close to, is beginning to suffer very badly with arthritis. She is becoming dependant on Penny to help with shopping, laundry and basic household chores. Her mother, always a source of strength and encouragement to Penny, is now becoming depressed and fretful about her increasing frailty.

At the other side of town, **Kate** is contemplating her own situation with a heavy heart: she has always enjoyed work and, until recently, got on well with her colleagues but her recent promotion meant moving into a different office where she feels very much the 'new girl'.

Her manager has told her bluntly that he wanted someone else for the job. He is making life very uncomfortable. He undermines her decisions and chips away at her confidence in a way that is both professionally humiliating and personally crushing. She fears she cannot continue like this and is seriously contemplating having to leave a job she loves.

In addition, her marriage has been going through a rocky patch—nothing serious, she hopes, but nevertheless, she senses an atmosphere at home. Her husband, Greg, thinks she does too much at church and was very angry recently when she took on yet another job that will demand more time away from the house. Kate understands his frustration but no-one else is offering. She has been talked into it because she has the skills needed. How can she say 'no'? The church needs her. Still, she feels guilty that another evening in the week is spent away from her husband and growing children.

Soul Workout

Life is not going well for Penny or Kate.

Penny's stress levels begin to reach crisis point after a nasty fall on black ice when x-rays reveal several broken bones. She will not be able to work for a while. She begins to fret about what is happening at work in her absence and whether she will still be in a job by the time she is fit enough to return. She is also feeling guilty about leaving her mother without the help she needs—even though a kind neighbour is doing the shopping and washing as needed.

Penny's thoughts are a jumble of anxiety and panic. Although she is an occasional churchgoer and believes in God, she would not describe herself as a spiritual person. At the moment her personal prayers don't stretch any further than 'Please God, get me better quickly. I can't afford to be off work and Mum needs me. Please keep my job safe. I'm sorry I'm not a good Christian: I promise to go to church more often when I'm back on my feet.'

Penny somehow thinks that she needs to bargain with God in order for him to help her.

Needless to say, her injuries take time to heal and her stress levels have hit the roof: she loses her temper at the slightest thing—her teenage children taking the brunt of her outbursts. She feels so guilty about letting her mother

Weight Resistance

down that she now dreads talking to her on the phone—despite her mother's reassurances that she is managing and that 'Sandra, next door, is taking good care of me.'

When Penny is finally well enough to take up her normal routine again she is hit by panic attacks at the thought of returning to work: she has convinced herself that she can't do the job, that her manager will see through her and she will be sacked. Going to work has become frightening. She begins to make excuses to stay away; she feigns illness and lies to cover up her real anxieties.

Relationships between Penny and her mother are at an all-time low: and it doesn't help that her mum keeps comparing her to Sandra. Penny has become deeply resentful of 'Sandra, next door' who, she believes is trying to muscle in and usurp her place with her mother.

She is anxious, angry, feels guilty and has lost all her self-confidence.

We could spend a lot of time analysing what is going on for Penny but it is sufficient for our purposes to say that she is weighed down by her burdens and feels defeated. She gives up trying to deal with them and doesn't resist the weight by finding ways through. *Penny has succumbed instead to the 'no-one understands' message of being a victim:* family, friends and colleagues are all

Soul Workout

blamed for her situation but above all she blames God who 'ignored' her prayers.

During this time **_Kate_** has also had to deal with some thorny issues but, as we shall see, with very different outcomes.

As with Penny, a crisis also pushes Kate into taking a back seat from her usual routine: for her it is the result of a smash in the car. During the same icy spell that has put Penny out of action, Kate's car has skidded out of control on black ice. Although the car has been written off, she has managed to avoid serious injury. She has severe bruising, whiplash injuries and has broken a bone in her wrist: in a lot of pain, she has been signed off work until further notice.

The difference in 'burden-management' between the two women has begun immediately: whereas Penny has gone straight into a severe and debilitating state of fretful anxiety, Kate's way of dealing with it has been to accept events for what they are: it hasn't stopped her being in pain but it is giving her 'time out' to rest, recuperate and reflect.

Kate's prayers have been formed around thanking God for protecting her from more serious injury, asking him to be with her in the pain, and help her get back on her feet as soon as possible. She has also asked God to use

Weight Resistance

this time of enforced rest to help her make the right decisions about her future.

Although in the past Kate has been a 'doer' she now has a sense that God wants her to just 'be'—even in the pain: this doesn't come naturally but she reckons that now is a good time to try out a different way. Anyway she reckons she can't do much to change the situation, so why fight against it?

As days go on, Kate is surprised that she is not fretting about who is doing her jobs—at work, church or home. Greg has taken on the cooking and Kate is managing to let him do it without being overly-critical of the less than perfect meals. Her daughter's enthusiasm for helping around the house has quickly waned but Kate reckons that life still goes on with a bit of dust—the housework will wait. Her son's cries of 'it's not fair' when asked to help are failing to make her feel guilty: 'they'll cope' is her predominant thought. That surprises her.

As for work, Kate is thanking God for 'time out' so that, between bouts of pain and sleep she can think about what she wants to do. At first she spent time silently shouting at God that a job she loved is now ruined but she has come through that and is now beginning to think about how to move forward. She decides that she wants to confront her manager about his bullying but she must do it in the right way; she resolves to talk it over

Soul Workout

with a trusted friend before deciding on any particular course of action.

Happy to leave it there for now, she somehow feels there has been some kind of a breakthrough, even though nothing has actually happened: it feels like she is taking some control over her own future.

Some days later, Kate is aware of a new thought creeping in to her conscious mind: supposing she decided to leave this particular job, what would she *want* to do? She is beginning to mull over what she enjoys and doesn't enjoy in the job (ignoring the problems posed by her bullying manager). Slowly her fragile self-confidence begins to grow stronger. For the first time she realises that she didn't really want the promotion. She only applied for it because her old boss had said she should be thinking of moving up the career ladder. Kate isn't really interested in 'career ladders' or the cut and thrust of higher management.

She has still a long way to go but is now thinking positively about work and, if she decides to leave, it will have less to do with her boss (though she isn't prepared to let him off the hook completely) and more to do with what she *wants*.

Likewise, she begins to see that Greg has got a point in terms of all the things she has got herself involved with at church. Despite her pain from the crash she is really enjoying a sense of being at home with her family: she had forgotten what it was like to relax or have a leisurely meal—she was always dashing from work to meetings, from meetings to the phone or emails: somewhere along the way life had stopped being enjoyable.

Kate is beginning to have an idea that maybe God doesn't need her to be constantly organising his affairs! Maybe, just maybe, he wants to have quality time with her as well. Certainly, in the peace and quiet of resting at home she has felt something stirring in her spirit: there is a warmth she can't quite describe but which feels energising, despite her physical pain.

As her health begins to improve she and Greg spend time walking in the countryside near their home—nothing very strenuous but they know something precious is happening. They are enjoying each other's company.

Kate is becoming aware that feeling the wind in her hair, looking at the rolling hills or listening to the sounds of birds, makes her feels closer to God than she has ever done before.

There are still issues to face, decisions to make about work and church commitments but the weight of these burdens feels lighter and more manageable because she feels connected—to her family, to God, to herself. Things will change because Kate herself is changing.

Kate is *resisting the weight* of her burdens by seeing possibilities where Penny sees only *im*possibilities. Kate has been helped to do this by asking for God's help rather than demanding that he sorts things out: her attitude to prayer enables her to ask God to show her *his* way of seeing things.

Penny's attitude to prayer has been to try to bribe the Almighty with promises of going to church more regularly and to become angry when he doesn't 'make things okay'.

She hasn't learnt that God cannot be bribed.

How to make use of weight-resistance principles in a Soul Workout:

Our two ladies are fictitious but yet I have heard snippets of this story told many times both inside and outside my counselling room. Penny and Kate are no different to most of us: we also struggle with problems and some of us will say 'the weight is too heavy, I can't carry it. It's all your fault,' whilst others will say 'Life is tough. I need to get on with it'—and some of us will add 'with God's help I will'.

This is where weight-resistance helps. By spending time prayerfully and being open to God's leading, we are allowing him to gently strengthen our inner

Weight Resistance

'muscles'. It may be that he gives us a different 'take' or understanding of our situation so that we can see the issue afresh and be able to find a way through; it may be that we find an inner courage or sense of peace that we didn't know we had and this increases our ability to cope; it may be that he shows us the next 'step' to dealing with the problem. It may also be that we come to a place of being able to accept the unchangeable and to find God and rays of light even in the darkest of places.

This is what is meant by balancing the weight: we will still be weight-bearing but we are not bowed down or injured by carrying our life-burdens.

Soul Workout offers a chance to come to God as if he were our personal fitness trainer and allow him to teach us how to exercise and tone our spiritual muscles for the burdens ahead.

But just a word of caution: remember I said earlier in this chapter that I have learnt not to use certain weight machines at the gym? My knees told me that it isn't a good idea to expect them to perform as well as an athletic twenty-year old. But not all the machines are beyond me: in fact there are some upper-body machines that I really enjoy.

The metaphor holds true for a Soul Workout too: sometimes we have to find alternative ways of doing the job.

Soul Workout

The exercises below are **suggestions** and may not be suitable for everyone. If you feel you just can't do it that way then listen to your intuition—don't feel that you have to persevere to do it in the way I have outlined: *my way is only one way.*

Make a decision instead to look for an alternative way to do the work.

For example, you may realise that you need to do some serious thinking and praying about your finances and so you bring it to the workout in the hope that God will show you the answer. None of the exercises suggested seem to touch the spot and you are feeling unfocussed and even confused by this.

Solution 1 would be to keep going in the hope that the light will eventually dawn (it may not).

Solution 2 would be to say 'this is all rubbish. I'm going to forget it' (the Soul Workout will go away but the financial problems probably won't)

Solution 3 would be to say 'I'm not getting anywhere with this. I need to find a different way to come at this problem.' It may be that you need to talk to someone—a financial advisor, perhaps—or to make some practical changes in your financial commitments. I'm afraid a Soul Workout can't do these things for you!

Resolving to tackle the problem in a different way will leave you open to spend your weight-resistance time on other issues. So, don't dismiss it because one life-burden is not material for a workout.

The cardiovascular work you have done earlier will strengthen you to take on this weight-resistance work. *I do not advise you to take on this aspect of the workout without first attending to your relationship with God.* This would be like positioning yourself incorrectly for the exercise you are about to undertake: you need to have the right posture (i.e. spending time with God first) to prevent spiritual injury.

SUGGESTED WEIGHT-RESISTANCE EXERCISES

As in the last chapter, there will be basic and advanced exercises offered and the initials will serve as a reminder as to which 'station' is covered by each.

However, life's burdens can be many and complex so you might find that doing one of the preliminary exercises outlined below will help you think in broad terms about what seems to be weighing most heavily on you at the moment. ***Only do one preliminary exercise***: if you are drawn to one in particular then do that; if not, then any one will do—they are all designed to help you begin to focus on priorities.

As before, don't try too hard: if you are beginning to struggle then put down the exercise and ask yourself what is making you feel like that. Use the **S.T.O.P.** acronym as outlined in the cardiovascular chapter and ask God to help you re-position so that you hold the right spiritual posture for the work you need to do.

Preliminary exercise 1

Think about the things you have done over the last week and how much time has been spent doing each thing. Remember that you are looking for a broad view here, so don't get bogged down with details of how you spent every minute: it is intended as an overall view of your life at the moment.

Now, in your journal make 3 columns:

Column 1: list the things you have done (at home, at work, or wherever you have been) because they are your responsibility—they may be in your job description or because only you can do them. Name them and broadly acknowledge how much time you have given them using the *Time Code* below*

Column 2: list the things you have done because you have wanted to do them but where you don't feel any sense of obligation. Hobbies and leisure activities come under this heading. Again, use the *Time Code* below*

Column 3 list all the other things you have done—it may include things you have taken on because you have felt unable to say 'no' or where you have given in because no-one else has come forward. It may include things that you have kept on, even though they have become superfluous—you just can't bear to let go. Keep to the *Time Code* below*.

*Time code: at the side of each activity record roughly how much time you have given using the scale indicated by the words:—

lot (a lot of time spent) ; **some** (less time but still a significant chunk) ;**little** (not much time spent on this) ; **Occasional**: acknowledge other activities you get involved in from time to time but which you didn't necessarily do last week.

Now look at the three columns and answer the following questions:

- How do I feel about what I have just done?

- Does it look as if my life is evenly weighted or does it seem out of balance?

Soul Workout

- Do I notice, or sense, that there is something in particular that is weighing me down?

- Is there anything from any of the columns that I would like to get rid of, reposition, or reschedule in terms of time?

At the moment you are only acknowledging these things as realities in your life. You can use this information to help you focus on real issues at the Stations.

Preliminary exercise 2

Answer the following questions in your journal & then place them in order of priority for working on . . .

- ➢ How strong do I think my personal relationships are? What might need to change?

- ➢ How easy do I find it to resist any negative thoughts and attitudes I might have?

- ➢ Do I feel that I need to work on improving my self-image and/or confidence?

- ➢ How strong am I in meeting the challenges of work? How might I become stronger?

> Am I happy with how I use my leisure time? What might I like to change?

> What do I want to give back to my church/community/society? How might I do that?

Preliminary exercise 3

Draw two circles to represent energy: one represents our *sources* of energy and the other circle represents our energy *drains*. Draw several spokes coming out of each: they represent specific sources or drains that you can identify within your life at the moment. Use the words in italics below to help you think about different areas of your life—there may be others you want to acknowledge as well.

family   *work*   *friends*   *hobbies*   *finances*
                  (paid or
                  voluntary)
social activities *church*   *spirituality* *community*

Try to be specific when filling in the spokes—for example, instead of writing 'family' on one of the spokes of the Sources of Energy circle, try to think what it is about family that energises you (perhaps you enjoy catching up over a family meal or enjoy relaxing together at weekends?).

Soul Workout

Note that the same things may appear on both circles for different reasons—for example, you may feel that family *drains* your energy as well as being a *source* of energy. Think what it is that drains you: perhaps there is a strained relationship in the family at present or maybe the morning rush to get everyone out of the house on time makes you feel tense every morning. Now look at the two circles and answer the following questions:

- How do I feel about what I have just done?

- Does it look as if my life is evenly weighted or does it seem out of balance?

- Do I notice, or sense, that there is something in particular that is weighing me down?

- Is there anything from either of the circles that I would like to change?

These preliminary exercises provide a general acknowledgement of how you are feeling at the present time. They are there only to note the weights and balances of your life before approaching the exercise stations where the real work begins.

Whatever exercise you decide to focus on, remember to *go with what draws you* rather than what you might feel comfortable with.

BASIC WEIGHT-RESISTANCE EXERCISES

a) **SS; JS**

Scriptures to spend time with: only take ONE reading—you can always look at the others on a different occasion—

- *Honouring God through our relationships—*
    Ruth 1 & 2: Ruth, Naomi and Boaz
    Matthew 5 v 21-34: A right attitude
    Matthew 7 v 1-5: Judging others
    Colossians 3 v 8-17: He is your life

- *In Service of Others—*
    John 13 v 4-17: Jesus washes the disciples' feet
    Luke 10 v 25-37: The Good Samaritan

- *Learning from our brothers and sisters—*
    Luke 10 v 38-42: Mary and Martha
    Luke 15 v 20-32: The Prodigal Son & his jealous brother

- *Be positive, not negative: Be satisfied, don't grumble—*
    Haggai 1 v 5-6

- *Anxious? Fearful?—*
    Luke 8 v 22-25: Jesus calms the storm.

As you read, be aware of how the passage might relate to you and your present circumstances. If a word or a phrase stands out then stay with it in the silence: allow thoughts to drop into your mind and prayerfully stay with what feels important. If, through your reading and reflections, you become aware of unresolved difficulties or burdens that feel weighty, ask God for wisdom and grace to bear with them until they are resolved.

You might like to review your reflections and insights in your journal: putting things down on paper can encourage further insight and deeper prayer.

b)   AS; JS

Using the circle exercise from earlier as a prompt, try expressing your sense of balance or imbalance as a picture representation: you might like to use colours to represent different feelings associated with your energy or lack of it. If there is significant imbalance then do a second representation of what you would want to change—maybe considering how you might be able to improve the situation

BUT REMEMBER that not everything can be changed: if this is the case, then talk with God about what you need to be able to accept and how you can manage your circumstances. Listen to any 'nudges' or inner promptings, as this may well be God talking to you. Keep your artwork, as it may prove helpful to you on further occasions.

Journal your observations.

c) AS; JS

We have different kinds of relationships with others and they all need attention and maintenance. Think of who you are, in relation to others in your life and express this by drawing a representation of yourself (a stickperson is sufficient), or writing your name on a page of your journal. Next, place others on the page, being mindful of where you put each in relation to yourself. If you are approaching this by drawing, you might also want the further symbolism of colour or size of representation to say something important about your relationships. Talk to God in the quietness of your own heart as you take note of anything needing particular attention and of your feelings, Journal your insights.

d) SS; JS

There is a myth that work is only work when it is paid! Actually we all work but some go out to do it (paid or unpaid) and others work at home—often

Soul Workout

unpaid! From washing the pots to making executive decisions we are all involved in work of some description.

Read the story of Mary and Martha in Luke 10 v 38-42 and then compare this with the parable of the workers in the vineyard (Matthew 20 v1-16). How do these two stories make you feel about whatever work you do? Reflect on your work (whatever it is and wherever it happens). Remind yourself of the highs and lows—what gives you energy and satisfaction and what drains you—you might like to represent this by drawing the circles from the Preliminary exercise again but, this time focussing completely on work issues. Don't fill up all your time with reading or writing—leave plenty of time for prayerful silence. Be open to God by accepting the thoughts that come: if they feel 'right' then stay with them—you may find a pattern emerging that leads to insight of a particular burden in your working life (remember how Kate used her 'time out' in the story earlier in this chapter?): this is one way that God speaks to us in the silence.

e) **JS; NS; AS**

If possible, take a slow stroll outside and allow your thoughts to move where they will within the parameters of your preliminary exercise. Be aware of

Weight Resistance

how you feel in relation to significant people in your life: consider different areas of life, such as family, friends, work, leisure, what you give back to society etc. As you walk, look for items in the vicinity that would express something of these thoughts and feelings. Use these items as 'visual aids' to help you talk to God about the weights you are aware of. Don't neglect to acknowledge how you are enabled to carry your life-burdens—even if this is only an awareness that you are able to carry on 'despite' the weight. As you walk, allow your thoughts to also recognize the areas of your life where there are no burdens—where life is light and easy, for it is important to hold the positive and negative in balance. Look for items in your walk to express this lightness.

At the end of your walk you may want to continue your reflections through writing or art. *(If you are not able to go outside for this exercise then look for items or pictures at the nature station that will stimulate your reflections)*

f) JS; NS

Take a slow stroll outside and, as you walk, *notice without judgement how you are feeling about yourself.* Notice whether you view yourself in a positive or negative way and talk to God about any negativity you are aware of. Allow yourself to see what you are good at and don't cause an imbalance in your life with false humility.

Humility is about seeing yourself as you really are—no better, no worse.

So thank God for the things you like about yourself. Offer your gifts and talents to him. Talk to him about the things you *don't* like about yourself and ask him for help to change these things—but remember that you need to be *willing* to change.

Use your senses as you walk and be aware of your surroundings.

Ask God to be with you and direct your thoughts: in this way you are working at both an outer level (what you see, hear etc.) and also at a deeper inner level (how do I feel about myself? Where is God in this?)

If you are inside, then I suggest you close your eyes and use the silence to do this work.

Leave some time at the end to journal your reflections and insights.

g) JS

Relationships can be the most wonderful part of life or they can make life hell. Be honest about your relationships and consider what you put into them—50% of the responsibility of making and maintaining relationships is ours (and equally, 50% is not!). As you write, hold each person in your mind as a silent prayer and talk to God about your feelings. Bring him in to your reflections about what needs to stay the same and what needs to change. Ask him to help you make changes where they are needed and to strengthen rocky relationships. Thank him for those relationships where you are loved and supported. Doing this in written form can help you put words to your feelings and enable you to identify the ups and downs of your relationships more clearly.

ADVANCED WEIGHT-RESISTANCE EXERCISES

a) SS; JS

Read 2 Corinthians 1 v 3-11 and 2 Corinthians 8 v 1-15.

What do these passages say to you about sharing, generosity and equality? Don't be tempted to turn this exercise into a theological or academic study

Soul Workout

but focus on what it says to you *personally* within the context of your life. What do YOU offer to family, friends, community, country, the church (in its widest sense)? What do you offer to God? *Be reflective and honest about **what** you offer and **how** you offer it:* for instance, if you offer your time, do you do it with joy and generosity or begrudgingly and with resentment? If you give to charity, do you do it as a heartfelt offering of love or as a way of easing your conscience? If you pray for others (intercessory prayer), do you do it out of duty or out of a deeply felt desire to bring that person or situation to God? Use your answers about *what* you offer to search out the truth of *why* you do it. Go easy on yourself—the *why* is often complex and convoluted: we are not perfect so there is likely to be some selfish or self-serving motives lurking around.

Note them without judging yourself.

The purpose of this exercise is not to heap on any guilt about what you do or don't offer or to blame yourself for less than altruistic motives and attitudes. The purpose is rather to dig deep into your soul to find who you really are, warts and all. God knows you through and through so you won't be shocking him, whatever you find.

Weight Resistance

Using the silence to connect with yourself as well as God can be scary and the temptation can be to skim the surface before quickly moving into a less threatening exercise. I encourage you, however, to stick with it, however uncomfortable it makes you feel: the discomfort will tell you something important about yourself.

Let God in and use your insights prayerfully. Firstly, in the silence thank God for the gifts of giving and sharing that he has made you aware of, however small or insignificant you may feel they are—for instance, you may not connect your smile and 'thank you' to a shop assistant as an act of 'giving' but both smile and words are offerings of appreciation: they make a difference.

Then *bring to God the things that you like about yourself*—including caring attitudes and positive ways you approach what you offer. Give thanks for them, for they are God's gift to you.

Some of your earlier reflections have been to look honestly at the things you don't like about yourself—things you *don't give or wrong attitudes*. Ask God to work with you to let go of these negatives in your life and replace them with positives. Notice that this is a two-way action: you and God in this process of change—you need to

Soul Workout

genuinely desire change and be willing to work at it: God can help you do this from the inside (your soul). This process is also about giving and offering!

b)   AS; JS; NS

Take a stroll outside, sit looking out of the window or use the resources from the nature station to help you focus. Spend a few minutes looking and noting what you observe either by briefly journaling it or by quickly sketching something you see.

Next, consider the following statement:

Nature gives to us without being asked and without waiting for permission for its times and seasons.

Reflect on the following: Spring, the season of emerging life and growth, can be likened to a season of taking up new challenges—perhaps becoming more active in your personal life, of volunteering, of becoming more involved with church or joining a pressure group.

Summer, a season of light, warmth and colour, can be likened to being fully involved in your giving and being happy and generous in doing so.

Weight Resistance

Autumn is a colourful and bountiful season but is, nevertheless, the last blaze of glory before winter. It can be likened to someone who is still giving and offering of themselves but who sense that they are beginning to tire and need to rethink how much they can continue to give in the future.

Winter is a season where little seems to be happening on the outside—but under the surface life continues by resting and preparing for the future. In life this can be viewed as taking a back seat and letting other people take the strain. In this context, winter is not necessarily old age or infirmity, but it describes a time in life when someone needs to rest and conserve strength for the future. It may describe a time when someone who has become 'burnt out' by being too busy needs to let go of the reins and recover from exhaustion; it could describe someone who has recently been bereaved and needs to grieve before considering the future or it could describe someone who has been debilitated by illness and who needs a period of convalescence.

What season are you in at the moment? Are you 'in a season' to offer your help or support somewhere? Or are you aware of this being a 'resting season'? Don't judge yourself, but accept how it is for you right now. Take note of how you

Soul Workout

feel and whether you sense any resistance to where you are at the moment.

Stay with these insights prayerfully and afterwards review how this exercise has made you feel.

c) **AS; JS; NS**

The following visualisation can be used side by side with the last exercise or used alone:

Sit quietly with your eyes closed and relax. Imagine you are in a garden or a wood where there are different kinds of trees (the landscape may be one you are familiar with in real life or purely a figment of your imagination) and give yourself a minute or two to look round your chosen landscape.

When you feel ready, choose one tree to stand or sit in front of. Take another minute or two to look around your chosen tree, noting how tall and broad it is and what season you are viewing your tree in.

Take a good look at the ***branches and foliage***: what do you see? Are there new leaves or blossom appearing? Is it in full leaf or is its foliage turning golden with autumn? Are the branches bare and stark? Stay with the foliage for a while: *recognise not just what you see but how you feel about what you see.*

Weight Resistance

Now look at the tree base: can you see any **roots** or are they completely hidden? Imagine that you can see them going down into the earth: do they go deep and provide a steady anchor when the winds blow or does it seem as if they run too shallow, providing inadequate stability and so risking the life of the tree in stormy times? Be aware of how this makes you feel.

Now consider the **bark surrounding the trunk of the tree:** do you get a sense of it being thick and gnarled with the years or is it thin, fragile and flaking off in places? Once again be aware of your reaction to what you see in your imagination.

Return to seeing the tree as a whole: is there a sense of strength or energy in your tree or does it bend over towards the ground, as if the weight it carries is too great? How does it feel to you?

After spending time with your tree prepare to return to the present: open your eyes, take a look around you and become aware of your surroundings. *When you are ready, journal or draw the tree you have just been visualising. This isn't about the art or your powers of description, it is about recording the visualisation so that you can go on to take the exercise one step further.*

Soul Workout

Now close your journal, *put your artwork behind you and move into the following reflection: you are now considering the tree from a totally different angle, for the tree is YOU.*

Roots: what keeps you anchored in life? Do your roots give you stability? Do they restrict your movement? What do your roots specifically refer to in your life? Who are the people and what are the events that have helped to form your roots? How do you relate and react to being rooted?

Bark: how well do you feel supported and held in the present? Who or what makes you feel secure at the moment? Who or what makes you feel vulnerable? How do these insights make you feel?

Branches: do you generally feel positive and able to hold your head up or do you feel bowed down, as if the weight is too much to bear? Who or what makes you feel this way? How does this play out in the way you live your life?

Foliage: do you feel that you are full of life, bursting with energy, like the foliage in spring or summer? Or, do you feel that life is an uphill struggle like the falling foliage of late autumn? Or does it feel like there is no foliage—a winter bareness lacking energy, vigour or vitality?

Weight Resistance

How do you feel about this?

Having reflected, return to your journal or artwork. Take a new page or piece of paper and, being careful not to refer to the first piece of work, draw or journal yourself as the tree.

Next, *compare the two pieces of work*: what similarities and differences are there? Can you see how the first part helped you get into the second?

What does this exercise tell you about the weights and burdens of your life?

If you feel overburdened, are there ways you may be able to make small changes to ease the weight? Be open to possibilities and remember that even the smallest of changes make for a lighter burden.

Use and review the exercise prayerfully. *Don't forget to review how you have felt about doing this exercise as this can also be a valuable insight into your inner self.*

For Group Leaders*:*

Once again the group will need you to unwrap the metaphor before they are ready to do the exercises. As before, the exercises are suggestions only: you may want

Soul Workout

to use them as they stand or adapt them to suit the group you are working with.

Because of the nature of the exercises it is possible that emotions may run high. It is important to let people feel what they feel and not to try to stop them.

There have been times when an individual has asked for some help during the exercise period. If this happens you need to be sensitive not only to the person but also to the occasion. If it is a quick question or small issue about the exercises it shouldn't be a problem and can be dealt with easily. But sometimes people come looking for more serious help. There are a couple of things to be careful of here:

1) Unless you are a trained counsellor please don't get into working with an individual on their 'problems'. Even if you are, this is not the best time and place to start any such work. If possible, and it seems appropriate, have some information about local counselling services to give to the person to follow up for themselves after the day. Whether they do or don't is their decision!

   The same holds true if you are a Spiritual Director.

2) It is important to 'hold the space' for everyone, so having lengthy discussions with anyone, especially where there is nowhere private to talk, can distract and disrupt other group members. Take the person to one side and offer to give them a little time at the end of the day—but make it clear that the above point holds! Do this in a way that is sensitive, respectful and affirming.

Chapter 10
Flexibility And Balance

Out of interest I looked in the Thesaurus for other expressions to use in case the word 'flexible' began to sound boring and here's what I came up with: supple, lithe, elastic, plastic (hmm, not sure I want to be seen as *that*), stretchy, bendable or bendy. The opposite of flexible is stiff—and, boy, is *that* one a pain! So, in the Thesaurus there are several words to describe how I want my body to be and one word to adequately describe the reality if I choose not to exercise.

I also looked up the word 'balance'—just to make sure I didn't tip over into ignorance—and came up with the following: equilibrium, poise, a sense of balance, stability and steadiness. The opposite is to be unsteady.

I'm still working on this one. Does anyone else have problems walking in a straight line? And, as for poise . . . . ?!

However, I am persevering.

One thing I *do* know is that perseverance, though sometimes hard and seemingly unrewarding, *does* pay off in the long term, even if it seems an uphill struggle at times. This is an aspect to explore in more detail when we begin to look at the spiritual implications of our metaphor.

When I entered a gym for the first time I was more aware of the daunting array of machines and weights than the area designated for floor exercises. Furthermore, when the fitness instructor gave me the initial tour she only gave me a very cursory explanation of what to expect in that area of the gym. My memory tells me that she was suitably vague about work to be done on 'the mat'—and, to be honest, I was more interested in the array of accessories stashed in the corner than in the realities of the exercise: large gym balls, hula-hoops and brightly coloured elastic straps took my attention. The large black mats hardly registered.

Little did I know that my body would soon have cause to fear the torture inflicted by these innocuous-looking mats. Nor did I understand the contortions required of my innocent limbs in order to justify a declaration of having completed this part of my workout. I was soon acquainted with the painful specifics of 'floor exercises'.

But I jest: I have come to respect the black mats and all they represent. It is quite some time since I thought of this part of my workout as torture—in fact I now enjoy it.

What a turn-around!

What I have come to appreciate is the fact that floor exercises keep my body flexible and balanced (or elastic and steady). Because my working life entails long periods of sitting down, I have needed to counteract my inertia with periods of movement: if I don't, I end up getting out of my chair in stages, making me feel much older than my years. A workout in general helps enormously but floor exercises have proved invaluable for my particular weak spots: my knees may not appreciate the weight-resistance machines but they really benefit from work done on the large black mat.

Floor exercises are lessons in determination; the hard work required to get my body to move with controlled smoothness as it stretches, bends and balances in repetitive sequences of challenging positions is not to be underestimated. Though push-ups are now beyond me, there are still many exercises to keep my back, arms, legs and knees on the move.

The accessories I mentioned earlier rarely feature in my routine: I occasionally have a go with the hula-hoop but, try as I might, I just cannot get it to do more than one

Flexibility And Balance

turn before it ends up round my ankles . . . . and I used to be so good at it too!

Essentially, with these exercises, it is just me and the mat. There is no machine to take the strain—or the blame. I lay on my back, on my front, sit up, kneel or stand as I stretch and bend, stretch and bend. Each position I adopt is designed to keep another part of me supple and on the go.

There is one Pilates position that is part of my routine: it aims to help me balance as well as stretch. I kneel on all fours so that my torso is parallel to the mat, my knees are in line with my hips and my hands (resting on the mat) are lined up with my shoulders. I then stretch out my left arm and right leg so that they are in a straight line with my body, and hold the position for a few seconds.

Then I bring them back into the resting position before moving my right arm and left leg in the same manoeuvre. And so on. By the time I have done several repetitions of the exercise I am beginning to waver and my sense of balance is decidedly shaky. I generally call it quits before I topple over.

The big, black mat is now my friend—but an exacting one.

Floor exercises can be summed up as '***stretch and bend with careful repetition***'; the secret is to keep going, even when your body would prefer to have a lovely soak in a warm bath—or, in my case, in the spa attached to the gym!

In just the same way we need to be spiritually flexible and balanced: by opening our spirits to God we enlarge our faith vision while staying stable and well-adjusted.

Having regular times to pray and read scripture may seem tough, especially when we lead busy lives or when we are tired and the repetition may leave us feeling numb with boredom or frustration. Having a 'Quiet Time' can sometimes feel like a desert experience where nothing seems to penetrate and nothing has meaning. Sometimes our prayers can feel like talking to thin air.

Take heart and join the club. Most of us would acknowledge these barren times—and don't believe the ones who say they never experience them.

The good news is that if you persevere you will begin to reap the benefits, even though it may feel like eternity before there is any obvious movement.

I have just returned from a gym workout and because my mind is tuned in at the moment to this part of the metaphor I was aware of what was happening for me and how I was feeling as I went through my routine on the mat. It was interesting to discover that I really *do* mean

Flexibility And Balance

what I say about having made the mat my friend: when I wrote it I used a bit of artistic licence, even though I knew my feelings had certainly undergone something of a transformation. However, this morning I noted the reality of arriving at this part of my workout with a sense of being in the right place, doing the right things: I felt satisfied that what I was doing had a purpose and meaning.

Why should I feel this way?

Because the familiarity of movement and the way my body was responding confirmed that the perseverance I have been talking about is paying off. I felt I was working together with my body, the mat and the routine rather than pushing against it in frustration. But this doesn't take away or negate the times I have really struggled. Believe me, there are many times I feel like saying 'I'll give it a miss today. I don't feel like it.'

Of course, there are always occasions when we give in and listen to the voice but if we listen too often we give up altogether.

Remember the phrase I used to sum up the floor exercises in the gym? Well, 'stretch and bend with careful repetition' can also sum up what we are talking about here.

How does it work on the spiritual level?

As you return to a set routine on a regular basis you begin to unlock new possibilities of being able to connect with God. The secret is to be 'stretchy' in your approach to scripture reading and prayer. Just as I move the sequence of my floor exercises around to provide variety, so by having several ways to approach your time with God (I call them Quiet Times) you minimise the boredom element.

But desert experiences are a natural part of the ebb and flow of spirituality and should not be seen as something going wrong. To give up at a low or 'barren' point in your spiritual experience is to give up on the natural order of your faith walk: persevere; be diligent, determined and stick with it. There are oases in deserts and there is no desert that goes on forever.

Like going to the gym, it is easy to say, 'I can't be bothered' or 'it's not working' when the going is tough but you will only reap the benefits if you keep working at it.

I don't know whether you have noticed but I've stopped talking about 'Soul Workout' at this point and begun to speak more generally about 'Quiet Times'? In some way the metaphor breaks down at this point: it is unlikely that you will want to do a full Soul Workout every week, so all my talk about the repetition of stretching and

Flexibility And Balance

bending may not seem relevant in this context. There is, however, a good reason for including it at this point: it is during a Workout that you may decide to ***try out*** different ways of reading scripture, praying and being with God.

I hope that by using these times of experiment you will find several approaches that you like and can connect with. When you do, I encourage you to take them into your day-to-day times with God—your 'Quiet Times'.

There are a number of suggestions to experiment with in the exercises at the end of this chapter. Some may be familiar to you, some may not, but try them; see what works for you; be open to new possibilities. Above all, be open to God saying to you, 'hey, I really feel like we have talked and listened to each other. I have really enjoyed the time we've shared.'

Can you imagine that this is what God might want to say to you?

Soul Workout

SUGGESTED FLEXIBILITY AND BALANCE EXERCISES

There is a different feel about the exercises in this chapter so, by all means, try out any suggestions that appeal to you ***but don't rule out the others:*** *this may be a time to experiment with the unfamiliar.* Remember my experience with the large black mat? To begin with I didn't want to have a go at the suggested floor exercises but, when I did, I found ones that suited me, that worked for me and that really do improve my flexibility and balance. I recommend that you keep an open mind and just have a go. Then, when you find ones that you feel you can work with (*note that I don't say 'ones you feel comfortable with'*) you can begin to build them into your more regular times with God. If there are ones you really can't get on with, then let them go: there are many 'floor exercises' but everyone finds the ones that work for them.

Because time is limited on a single workout day, I suggest that you use the last 30 minutes before returning to the group for the 'Cool Down' to try ***one*** exercise. You can try others on different occasions, when time is not pressing.

Flexibility And Balance

If, however, you are doing the workout over a number of sessions, then this 'floor work' can be seen as one whole session and more time given to it accordingly.

BASIC FLEXIBILITY AND BALANCE EXERCISES

a)   SS

The scripture references below focus on some words I have used repetitively through this chapter. Choose one reading, or, at most, one category . . . As you read, you may want to stay with one particular word or phrase ***(Lectio Divina)***. Sit with it; repeat it; open your mind to how this impacts on you, and on your life. Let God speak to you through it.

- *Perseverance* Romans 5 v 1-6
  2 Thessalonians 1 v 3-4
  Hebrews 12 v 1-3
  James 1 v 2-4

- *Balances*   Proverbs 16 v 11

- *Diligence*   2 Chronicles 24 v 12-13
  Romans 12 v 7-9
  1 Timothy 4 v 14-16

- *Reading of Scripture* Psalm 119 v 105

b) AS; JS

With pastel, paint or any other art medium to hand, *quickly draw a series of random closed shapes on your paper* (squares, ovals, triangles etc.) Draw them in any way you like and wherever on the page you want, using any colour you fancy. Now spend time reflecting on how you have approached and completed the exercise (you might like to record these reflections in your journal): how did you arrive at the completed page?

Did you read what was written and get on with it straight away?

Did you take time to think about how you were going to do it?

Were there shapes you repeated? Were there shapes you left out deliberately? Where have you placed them on the page? Do they cover the page evenly or are they skewed to one side? Are all the shapes a similar size or do the sizes vary?

As you take time to consider these questions also consider whether they remind you of anything in your life: can you name them? Do they have any relationship to each other? If you were to draw

Flexibility And Balance

a line to connect them, where would you start and finish? Would they all be connected or would some shapes be left out? Why?

Out of this exercise what would you want to say to God? Have you any sense of His reply? Do you need to do anything more to the shapes on the page or are they complete as they are? Take your time with this exercise. Don't rush it. Be open to any thoughts that present themselves.

c) **NS; JS**

Pick a photograph, picture or object to use for this reflective exercise:

—Or, you might like to go outside to look for a natural object to contemplate.

Now sit with it. Look—*really* look at it: see the whole picture / object but also pay attention to the detail. If it is an object, then pick it up and handle it: close your eyes as you do this so that you really *feel* it.

Allow your emotions to open up. If you notice any strong emotions don't close them down but invite God into them. *Stay with your picture or object for some time: this can be a real test of determination and perseverance.*

Do you notice anything changing as you remain with your chosen icon?

Do you have any sense of it pointing to an important truth or insight?

Journal your insights.

d) NS; JS

Sometimes we need to just 'BE':

During this exercise you may learn something about perseverance.

First of all, (if you can) look through the window or go to the outside door: take notice of the season and the weather. If I say 'do you want to go outside?' notice how you feel about my suggestion: do you feel that, whatever the weather, you want to do it? Do you react with 'if it was warmer/dryer/lighter I would' or 'I would if I could.' Be aware of your initial reactions.

If you can go outside, *and you want to*, find a place to sit for a time: if you are staying in, draw up a

Flexibility And Balance

chair near the window so that you have a view of the outside.

Now SIT. Just that. Nothing more.

Let your senses loose. In terms of flexibility and balance this is about noticing what is around you so that you can 'ground' yourself, wherever you are. Whether you see garden, buildings or concrete, be aware of the details. It may be a familiar scene or a completely new one. Wherever you find yourself at this moment, sit with it. You may be surprised how much you have taken for granted or have completely missed. If the scene is familiar, notice whether anything has changed since last you looked or if not, allow yourself to enjoy revisiting the familiar. The scene in front of you may be well-loved but, for some of you, it may bring feelings of dissatisfaction, unease or plain dislike. Whatever your feelings, be aware of them and ask God to share these moments with you.

Then, with God and in acceptance of reality, just BE there. The time you take doing this is up to you but stretch it into a period rather than a moment.

As you sit, be observant of yourself as well as your surroundings and be open to any insights or specific threads or patterns.

Soul Workout

After you have sat for a period of time and you feel the exercise is at an end, there is one more thing to do: review how you have approached and completed the exercise: Review in a prayerful way. If you decide to journal your review then make sure you don't do this until you have gone back inside or changed your position or you may be tempted to cut the exercise short in favour of writing.

e) **SS**

If you use daily Bible reading notes, a Lectionary or the Daily Office you might feel you want to use them in this period of the day. It is important for some people to feel they are connected with others of the same tradition as they pray. Using these set readings and prayers may help you find a workable discipline for regular times with God. It is essential that you read slowly to digest the meaning. Pray from the heart, even if you are reading the words. Remember that sometimes the going will get tough but persevere and determine to stay with it: spiritual suppleness and equilibrium are to be found through perseverance.

f) **JS**

Write about your hopes and dreams: what are you looking for in life? Where do you hope to be in a

Flexibility And Balance

few years' time? What skills do you feel you have, or need? What interests do you want to pursue? How do you want your life to look in a few years' time?

When you have done this, spend some time looking at what needs to grow and what needs to die away in your life for some of these dreams to come to fruition. S-T-R-E-T-C-H your mind—don't be content to take a back seat in your own life. Balance what may be feasible and what is pie-in-the-sky. But, be careful not to dismiss things as unattainable without due consideration. Try to bend your mind around some of the obstacles to see what is possible and then be determined to pursue your goal to its natural conclusion: for some things opportunities will open up but others will reach dead ends. That is life.

Be sure to include God in all of your thinking—he wants to be on the inside of your life and not just an occasional extra.

g) AS; JS

Stretch yourself by writing a poem to express something important in your life—it may not be about anything specifically spiritual but needs to be something that is on your mind at the moment. *Note:* some poems rhyme and some use rhythm

Soul Workout

to hold them together and some use a much freer style—this isn't an English assignment so feel free to write as you are led: the aim is to be enabled to express yourself, rather than to write a technically perfect poem. Read it back: does it say what you want it to say?

How do you feel about having written it?

If you want to take this a step further, try illustrating the poem with some of your own artwork. Keep it simple—and remember that no-one else needs to see it.

You may not have enough time for all of this exercise—start it now and finish it at a later time if you wish.

ADVANCED FLEXIBILITY AND BALANCE EXERCISES

a) **SS**

Centring Prayer: this is an ancient form of prayer. It makes use of a contemplative attitude by focusing on a particular word, using it like a mantra. Jesus, Yahweh, Abba, Peace are all commonly used words to focus on.

Flexibility And Balance

To begin with it may be helpful to choose a simple Bible verse. Suggested verses (though this is by no means an exhaustive list):

Psalm 23 v 1; Psalm 37 v 7; Psalm 119 v 105; Isaiah 55 v 6; John 1 v 1; John 3 v 16

Choose only one verse.

Then proceed as follows:

Find a comfortable position, so that you are not shuffling around, and spend a few moments stilling your body. Read your chosen verse over slowly and repeat several times. There may be a word from this reading you want to use as a mantra but, if not, then consider using one of the words above.

Focus on your breathing so that you are breathing deeply and slowly but without discomfort. As you breathe in say the first part of your mantra (YAH . . .); as you breathe out complete your mantra (WEH); (*or* JE . . . SUS; *or* PEA . . . . CE.)

It can be done very quietly out loud, if you are sure you won't disturb anyone else or you can say it silently. Keep going with your chosen word.

Soul Workout

In Centring prayer you are not encouraged to follow threads of thinking but to empty your head of thought by the repetitive use of the word. Its power is in allowing you to be open and present to God without distraction. If you notice your mind wandering, then return to your chosen word. Say it slowly and continue to repeat it until you reach a place of total stillness and silence. Continue in this manner for 10-20 minutes—longer is better if you can manage it.

b) NS

Take a gentle walk or go and sit outside if possible. If not, try to sit by a window so that you can look out. Observe, note and check out the world around you, taking note of *how things look:* do you see life and energy in the things around you or do you see a time of apparent barrenness? Winter can look barren because nothing much appears to be growing but summer can also, surprisingly, look barren when there is a heat wave or a drought: the land looks parched and bare and the plants take on a dull, listless look.

Maybe you see something between the two—a transition period?

Flexibility And Balance

Walking or sitting, take time to relax your body and mind so that you can be attentive to the rest of the exercise. Don't rush.

As you look at the outside world, *begin to move inside, finding connections with your soul.* Does what you are looking at on the outside have any resonance with the season of your spiritual life at the moment? Or is it showing you the direct opposite of how things are spiritually?

Don't question or challenge your insights but accept that 'this is how it is'. Reflect on other times when it has felt similar and yet other times when your faith walk has been in a very different season. Accept all as 'being as it has been'.

This is the steadiness (BALANCE) of being at ease with whatever life offers—highs and lows.

BEND your mind and memories back to feel how it felt then and to re-experience your spiritual journey. Be honest and go deep. Recognise and acknowledge the times when you have felt 'cold' towards God, or disappointed or even angry with him: don't worry—he already knows these truths about us and he can (and does) handle our emotions, whatever they are.

Soul Workout

It is equally important to re-experience those times of 'warmth': deep joy and love to be found when feeling very close to God.

Seasons and transition times of the soul are as much a reality as those within nature.

STRETCH yourself to look at possibilities for the future: if you are in desolate place at the moment, might these exercises open you to new spiritual growth? If you are in a place of rich growth, how might this be expressed in the nitty-gritty of everyday life?

Consider the exercises you have done in this Soul Workout: are there ones you want to continue with by yourself after the day is over? Or others you have not been able to do on the day that you want to try?

Ask God to open up the possibilities to you.

BE FLEXIBLE in the way you approach prayer: some ways of praying have been looked at in the exercises today, but there are many other ways to pray.

One of my favourite forms of prayer I call 'Arrow Prayers': I talk to God in my head as I go about daily life—nothing fancy, just really an extension of my thinking—but it makes me feel as if I am

Flexibility And Balance

including God in the nitty-gritty of my day. There is no beginning or end to my arrow prayers: I generally refer to God as Lord, Father or Jesus, but that is a personal choice. It doesn't replace quiet times of prayer but is merely a different expression of prayer. As you walk or sit, consider how YOU can be flexible in your prayers.

Look at ways to encourage yourself when the going gets tough. Be practical as you consider these possibilities: time to read a few verses of your Bible and end with a short prayer may be all you can give on a regular basis right now but, if so, PERSEVERE. Better to have a few minutes regularly than to look in vain for time you can't give—that way risks a bleaker soulscape. When you persevere it then makes it easier to go deeper when life is less difficult.

End this exercise by repeating the words

BALANCE, BEND, STRETCH, BE FLEXIBLE, PERSEVERE.

These words will act as an 'aide memoire'.

c) **SS; JS**

Take a favourite story from the Bible and rewrite it as if it was happening now. You might like to put a journalistic slant on it, as if you are reporting a breaking news item. When you have finished, read it back to yourself. Does it give you any insights into the background of the story? Does it give you any clues as to why that particular story was included in the Bible—what was the writer trying to convey to his readers? Does it reveal anything about your own journey? Does it extend your understanding or show you aspects to a familiar passage that you hadn't seen before? Finally, re-read the original passage in the Bible. This puts it back into context but allows your new insights to breathe life into it.

For Group Leaders:

In some ways this is the hardest section of all, as people will be beginning to tire. Decide before the day if you are going to include this section. If you are doing the workout over a number of meetings this would fit neatly as a 'stand alone' session (just like a Pilates class in metaphorical terms).

Including it in a full day means that you need to tag on about 30-40 minutes at the end of the weight resistance work: to make the day flow more smoothly try offering a handout with the metaphor explained along with the suggested exercises—then people don't need to regroup until the Cool Down period. Make these sheets available before or during the weight resistance period so that people can organise their own time. As long as they are made aware at the beginning of the day (perhaps with a reminder in the programme sheet) then this section can flow from work already done.

As a 'stand alone' session the metaphor is better explained verbally and more time can be given to the exercises. A session taken from this section could be offered to churches, housegroups, or cell groups as a Taster session.

Chapter 11
Cooling Down

It can be really tempting at this point in a workout to breathe a sigh of relief and leg it as quickly as possible back to the changing room.

BIG MISTAKE!

It may seem as if your hard work is all over: your face is red, your skin is like a colander with the perspiration leaking out and you are looking forward to having a shower to freshen up. All that is very understandable but, neglect this final routine, and you are likely to suffer. Aches, strains and injury result from a sudden stop. Better to spend a few moments stretching all the muscle groups throughout your body so that they can wind down gently.

It only takes a few minutes.

I can hear some of you fidgeting as you look at your watch and wonder what on earth this has to do with a Soul Workout: there's no red sweaty face when the workout has been spiritual and there's nowhere for a shower, even though it would be very refreshing. You've done your workout, you're tired and realise that you are nearly out of time. Surely you can just pack everything away and go home, pick the children up from school or put the tea on?

Well, yes you could. But the transition from silence to noise, unhurried to rushed, and reflective to active is not as easy as it may seem. A few minutes on a Cool Down will help you to go back to your everyday routine feeling refreshed, recharged, energised and ready to face life.

People doing the workout alone *will find a few suggestions for cool down exercises at the end of this chapter.*

A word to group leaders: this is the point when everyone gathers together again to round off the day. Most of the time has been spent with people working quietly and alone; they have been involved with their own stories and their own inner and outer lives. The space you now offer to the group needs to retain a sense of quiet trust that will honour the depth of spirit touched by them during the day.

It can be helpful and less intimidating to come into a room with quiet music playing in the background than

Soul Workout

to re-assemble in complete silence. However, it is more important that *you* hold the stillness and silence for the group as you wait for everyone to arrive. By sitting quietly relaxed you will send a message to the group that it isn't a time to chat. The Cool Down is a time to ease spiritual muscles so that participants can return to the world and their everyday lives without difficulty.

I have suggested a couple of alternative cool down exercises for the group below.

Use only one.

SUGGESTIONS FOR A GROUP COOL DOWN EXERCISE

1) Before the group gather, place an unlit candle on a table, providing a focal point for the group (a pillar candle works best). Leave the rest of the table free. Place a tea-light on each chair.

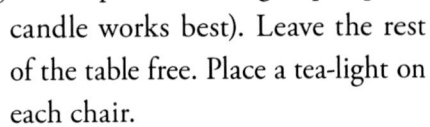

   When the group have assembled and are settled offer a quick summing up of the day—nothing lengthy: a sentence for each section of the programme will suffice. Acknowledge the way the group have approached the workout and

Cooling Down

affirm their hard work. Explain the importance of the Cool Down.

Then, in silence, or with some quiet, reflective music playing, give them a few minutes to think about the day: what had been their initial hopes and fears? How has their day worked out for them? What have they focussed on? How are they feeling now? ***Is there a word or phrase that sums up what the workout has meant to them?*** (This is something for you to do as well—you have also been involved in the day, albeit in a different role) Ask them to hold the word in their minds.

After a few minutes of silent review, it is time for you to light the main candle: as you do this, offer your word, as a gift. Before sitting down, open up the gift by suggesting that they come to the table, light their candle and place it with yours. Suggest they speak their word out if they would like to share it with the group: the spoken word has more power than a thought.

Sit with the lit candles for a few minutes: give thanks to God silently for time spent with him, yourself and each other during the day.

At the end of this period there needs to be a definite ending and letting go of the day: as group leader

Soul Workout

this is a role given to you. A short poem, a blessing or a short prayer is all it needs.

The Cool down is now ended.

2) **Suggest that people might want to bring** with them a piece of art work or writing they have done on the day: (the idea is best introduced at the *beginning of the day* and reiterated at this point) make clear that there is an alternative of bringing an object they have used during the day—a pebble, leaf, feather etc. Be sure to clarify that no explanation will be asked for and there will be no public viewing of personal work. The purpose of bringing these items is to have them as a visual reminder of the day.

If possible, it is best to sit in a circle for this exercise but it isn't essential.

As they come in ask them to place their items on the floor in front of them.

When the group have assembled and are settled, offer a quick summing up of the day—nothing lengthy: a sentence for each section of the programme will suffice. Acknowledge the way the group have approached the workout and affirm the importance of the items they

Cooling Down

have brought back with them. Explain the importance of the Cool Down.

Then, in silence, or with some quiet, reflective music playing, give them a few minutes to think about the work or item they have brought back into this space: what have they brought? Why this particular piece or item? What, if any, insight has it given them? How might they be able to use it to develop further insights? Has this work touched any deep issues that may need further work? Have they any ideas on how to proceed with this? What will they do with any artwork or writing after the day has finished? What has the day meant to them? How are they feeling as they approach the end of the day?

When this time of silent review is over, there is a need to let go of the day and it needs to be done in a way that affirms the group as well as the individual.

As leader, turn to the person at your side and offer a word of blessing: this is a blessing that each person in the group is going to offer in turn to the person next to them until it reaches you again. You are the first to offer it and the last to receive it.

Keep it simple. Suggestions are:

'May the God of peace go with you';

'Peace and blessing be yours';

'Go in peace'.

Or, if you want to make it more pertinent to the day, try 'thank you for sharing this day with me'.

Whatever blessing you choose, give each person space to receive and offer it without being rushed.

When it has been offered back to you the cool down is complete.

Before closing, there are some important pointers for the future to offer to participants. In preparation you need to have read the chapters on Back in the Changing Room and Hanging on to the Feel-Good Factor. Keep any verbal pointers for the future short: give people chance to take information away on handouts: they will be tired at this point and some will need to get home for family commitments. Better to give them something written as a reminder, than that they forget something important.

You can then dismiss the group. The day is complete.

Some Suggestions for your personal Cool Down (if you are working out alone)

Choose one of the following options:

1. Take a few minutes to review all that you have done in your workout. This is not so much an in-depth appraisal as an impression of how the time has been spent: have you sat throughout? Been outside some of the time? Done some artwork or written in a journal? Have you meditated or used your imagination in any of the exercises? Has time seemed to fly or has it dragged? How has your workout left you feeling?

By doing this you are giving yourself permission to let it be what it was (without feeling the need to make it less or more than it has been) and to let it go in order to pick up on normal life again.

As you review, make a note of anything you want to return to at a later date—maybe something has connected at a deep level and you feel it needs further exploration. Or perhaps you have become aware that you need to talk to someone about an issue that has come up. It is important that you only *note* this at the moment: deciding what to do and who to talk to is another matter and one I shall touch on in the next chapter.

When you have finished your review, gather all your materials together and put them out of sight: *your Cool Down is now complete*—no need to keep going back to it. You will not lose anything by doing this because God will remind you of anything significant in due course. Trust him.

2. **Gather your workout material in front of you**—pictures, journal and anything you have spent time with while on your journey through different Stations. Make a space in the centre and light a candle. Pick up one of your gathered objects and, in a sentence, thank God for the specific work you have done with the help of that item, acknowledging any insight it has given you. Once you have done this, place the item behind you and pick up another from in front of you. Repeat the process until all the objects are behind you. End with an 'Amen' as you blow the candle out.

Now your Cool Down is over.

Cooling Down

Please only attempt this Optional Cool Down if physically able to do it without causing strain or injury.

3. If your workout has led to you sit for quite a long time and you have not had chance to stretch your legs then I suggest you use your Cool Down time to do this. Take off your shoes. Stand straight and tall by imagining a piece of thread coming from above the centre of your head, and going right through the centre of your body to the floor between your feet; this thread is gently pulling your head so that you are looking straight in front of you; it is keeping your chin up, your shoulders back, your arms by your side, your hips straight, your feet together and flat on the ground. This thread now pulls you up gently on to your toes. It keeps you there a few seconds and then slackens enough for you to return to standing with both feet flat to the floor. Repeat twice more.

Now bring both arms round from your sides in an arc until they are pointing straight to the ceiling on each side of your head; as you do this, keep your head straight and your eyes looking straight in front of you. Raise your heels from the floor so you are on tiptoe. Reach up as high as you can before bringing your heels down so you are standing flat on the

Soul Workout

floor again. Bring your arms back down in an arc to rest at your sides. Repeat twice more.

Put your hands on your hips and gently twist your upper body to the left while keeping your feet firmly on the floor; return to the centre before twisting your body to the right in the same way. Repeat twice more.

Return to the centre and let your hands hang loose at your sides. To finish, gently shake out each leg and foot and each arm and hand in turn until they are loose and relaxed.

Now your Cool Down is over.

Chapter 12
Back In The Changing Room

At the beginning of this book I said that arriving at the gym always gives me a sense of satisfaction that I haven't given in to the little voice whispering 'don't go today'? But I also expressed a sense of fear because gym changing rooms hold disagreeable school memories for me:

Well, here we are again, back in the place where it all started.

But this time I go through the changing room door with a different mixture of emotions . . . .

I feel a tremendous **sense of fulfilment** that I have actually done it; I have been disciplined enough to get to the gym and determined enough to see my workout through. Somehow I can never quite believe that I am capable of it.

Soul Workout

I feel **energised** but at the same time I also feel **tired**, as befits having worked hard.

I am aware of being hot and sweaty and this makes me feel **a little uncomfortable**: I can't wait to get out of my sweaty clothes and into something clean and fresh.

Lastly, I am aware of a **sense of completion** and that it is time to move on and out; time to get on with whatever the day holds.

Do any of these statements resonate with you after your Soul Workout? Even the bit about being hot and sweaty may echo with your sense of effort, depth of thought and struggle to remain focussed. Doing a workout is not easy.

People in gyms vary: some choose not to use the changing rooms at all, preferring to go home to shower and change, but most do. There is something about using a changing room that carries an implication about our ability to leave the workout behind—but more about that in a minute.

Remember that in an earlier chapter I said that a changing room provides a physical and psychological boundary between the outside and the gym itself? It is both a protection from outside distraction and a focus of preparation for work to be done.

Back In The Changing Room

There is a subtle difference between this and returning after exercising: it works the other way round. The changing room still acts as a boundary but now it *enables us to move from the gym to the outside.* It is the place where we put aside our gym clothes, freshen up and get ready to face the rest of the day. What we wear may look similar—trousers, t-shirt, trainers—but when we haven't worked out in them they will feel fresh.

In terms of our Soul Workout it is important that we 'change gear'—not clothes this time but a psychological shift of purpose. We have done our exercises, we have set that time apart and now it is time to say goodbye to it.

It is not too much of a metaphorical leap to say that if we were to stay in the same 'gear' once we leave our 'set-aside time' behind we may end up getting the cold shoulder and being rebuffed by people we meet: in terms of the metaphor, we would not 'smell' good to people.

Why?

Because if we don't give ourselves a way to return to the thoughts, words and actions of everyday life it will be harder to focus on routine jobs and mundane conversations.

The end of a workout can leave us so full of impressions, depth of insight, enthusiasm or sense of purpose that we find it hard to cook the tea, chat to the assistant at the

Soul Workout

supermarket check-out or deal with squabbling children. It can be hard to connect with others who have not been on the journey with us and they might misinterpret our manner as being arrogant, ignorant, condescending or patronising.

Coming directly away from a workout without visiting the changing room first can leave us struggling to communicate anything at all. The silence or depth of inner work can make noise and superficial things seem like intrusions into our more 'mystical' world: for a time in the workout the Mystery of Spirit can seem more real than the physical world we generally inhabit. There can be a reluctance to return to everyday life. But we are a composite of physical, psychological and spiritual and there is a need to set time aside for all aspects of who we are.

Other people may not share our sense of mystery or spirit but the changing room, as I have said before, is a great leveller. It gives us chance to readjust ourselves so that we can function within the 'worldly' side of ourselves and not be seen as 'other-worldly'. It doesn't honour God for us to be seen as so super-spiritual that we are unable to have normal conversations or live in harmony with others.

We may need to visit the changing room to let go of the silence and all that has gone with it and put on a garment of 'ordinariness' with which to re-enter the world.

On the other hand we may be longing to tell the next person we meet all about our workout. If we rush to share any insights they might be taken aback by the intensity or depth of them and so they might make light of them or miss the point of what we are trying to say. This can take the edge off what has been important to us and so run the risk of spoiling our enthusiasm.

I am not saying that we shouldn't share *anything* but perhaps there are more appropriate times to share at depth than immediately after we draw the workout to a close. It is better to give space and time to whatever comes next and save any sharing until we have re-established ourselves back in our ordinary lives.

I am labouring this point for two reasons:

- It is *our* journey and not the other person's. We expect too much if we think they can come in 'coldly' on our insights with the same understanding and intensity. We might need to take time in our explanation or to give some background to our insights. If we rush in, as we might be tempted to do, we are trying to get them to the same place we are at—but they haven't done the exercise! They are unlikely to 'get it'.

- Things can be said that might be regretted later on. Sometimes, in the heat of just having finished, personal things may be shared with the wrong person, or *too much* is shared, making us vulnerable: once said it cannot be taken back. It is better to let a bit of time lapse before anything of significance is shared. Getting back into the ordinary routine of life can have a stabilising effect so that what we share and with whom is done in a more measured way and with more wisdom.

There is a time to work out and a time to finish.

So, how do we 'change gear' when we have worked out alone?

The time spent 'in the changing room' will be different for everyone but it should not take longer than fifteen minutes for anyone.

When we were getting ourselves ready in the changing room at the beginning, I made a point of suggesting that all distractions such as telephones and computers were switched off and the door was locked against unexpected visitors.

Now I am suggesting that you reverse the process:

- ❖ Switch the phone on; put the computer on if you would normally have it on (but not otherwise)

Back In The Changing Room

and unlock the door (if you would normally have it locked I suggest that you unlock it as a symbolic action and then re-lock it as a sign that life has returned to normal).

These are gestures to signify that you are ready to let the world in.

- ❖ If you have been in silence throughout the workout I suggest you put some music on quietly, just to 'lift' the silence *or* if you have already used music, try a change of tempo and play something with a bit more beat, or have it on slightly louder (but not *too* loud). For anyone who has used music for much of the workout, try turning it off and enjoy the silence.

- ❖ There may well be a number of objects on the floor or table from work you have done at the 'stations': now is the time to put them away—or, if that would take too long or be too difficult, then put them together in a cupboard or in a room where you will not be tempted to go back and start again.

- ❖ Don't throw any artwork or writing away just yet, as you may want to return to them in your regular time with God. Resist any impulse to add or take away from what is done. Store them in a safe place, free from prying eyes (including your own). You will know where to find them if necessary.

❖ Some people find it a good idea to do something practical: wash the cup you have been using; straighten the throw on the chair; open the window; wash your face, brush your hair or apply makeup prior to going out; change your shoes.

As part of 'changing gear' you need to become mindful of what plans you have for the period immediately following. By doing this you are beginning to move away from the workout and preparing to re-join life—and life has a habit of not being quite as calm and peaceful as the workout has been. Being thrown into the hurly-burly of life as soon as you walk out of the door or when the first member of the family returns home can be tough—but having taken off your 'gym clothes' you are now as ready to get back into life as you will ever be.

For Group Leaders

How do we 'change gear' in a group?

It would be helpful if people were offered a short explanation of what to expect as they leave: I have already dealt with this at the end of the last chapter so it needs no further comment, except to say, that in many ways it is relatively easy for people in a group to move through this transition: coffee may be served at the venue, offering people chance to talk before leaving—though be wary of any in-depth discussion about the day. Coats may need to be put on, bags sorted out, toilets visited and cars manoeuvred or buses waited for and journeys completed. All these offer a transition from the soul workout space to everyday life.

Part Three
Leaving The Workout Behind

Chapter 13
Hanging On To The Feel-Good Factor

So, now it's done. The workout is over.

You are ready to return to normal life—hopefully with an added spring in your step.

When a gym workout is complete people generally experience a rise in the 'feel good' chemicals called endorphins. These flood our bodies and help us to fight infection and illness. But they are not only produced by physical exercise, for these chemicals can also be released by being relaxed and inwardly positive—as I hope you are feeling at this point.

Experiencing this 'feel good factor' after your workout is an added bonus to be enjoyed for as long as it lasts.

But it doesn't last forever and for some it won't last long at all. For some, coming to the end of the workout will produce mixed feelings because, for them, returning to daily life will be stressful: all manner of difficulties may be waiting and they know that it won't be long before they are back into the very heart of the burdens they have been dealing with in their weight resistance work.

Life sometimes has big anxieties—hard issues—such as marital tensions, problems with the children, loneliness, work pressures, unemployment, financial hardship, health or other complex concerns. Most will refuse to disappear on their own and our natural inclination may be to run away, to pretend they're not there. But we need to stand and face them squarely—and that can be easier said than done.

The good thing about doing a Soul Workout is that it can help to keep us strong within these difficult situations: although the workout itself has been 'time out' the results can be very practical and grounding. The work not only encourages a healthy relationship with God but also strengthens us to face difficulties, whatever they are.

When we live closer to God we find that our priorities shift and we begin to look at things differently.

We often find an inner courage to make changes and experience an inner peace that is not dependant on external circumstances. Sometimes the change is a new-found ability to accept what is unchangeable.

Of course, these inner changes will not *solve* problems but they can make the difference between moving forwards and sinking under the weight.

So, when the Workout is over *and it is time to get on with the rest of life, how do you hang on to that sense of having done something worthwhile?*

Here are some suggestions:

- ➢ Remember that, no matter what happens, what you experienced in your workout was real. Any insights you gained; any sense of drawing close to God; anything you wrote or expressed creatively or any feelings of calmness and peace remain real, even though the moment has passed. Accept them.

- ➢ Don't strive to make everything right. Accept that you only have limited abilities to sort out the 'mess' of life. Be realistic about what you can do or take on: don't think that the workout will turn you into a super-hero. Deal with those things you need to and let God sort out the rest. Remember the preliminary exercises from the chapter on weight-resistance.

- It is helpful to be able to share with someone you trust but don't expect everyone to understand what you have been doing on your workout. Be wise in choosing who you share with and when.

- Enter fully into life and be mindful of what you are doing, giving your whole attention to it. Just because it isn't 'spiritual' doesn't mean that it isn't of God.

- Look for God in the ordinary things of life: people like St Ignatius and St Francis experienced God everywhere and lived accordingly. We can do the same. Live by the axiom 'God in all things'. You may be surprised where you bump into him!

- If, as part of your workout, you resolved to do something, then do it as soon as is practical. The longer you leave it, the more likely you are to forget or lose courage.

- The workout is designed to keep all aspects of your inner life healthy and should not be seen in isolation. Give yourself permission to review how things are going in a few weeks: have you noticed any shifts or differences as a result of doing the workout? Be honest: if there is change then acknowledge it; if there is no apparent movement

Hanging On To The Feel-Good Factor

then acknowledge that also. Be honest about how you feel. Is there anything you need to go back to? Perhaps it feels like unfinished business or maybe something has changed and you need to make some other adjustments? Do you need to look at doing some of the exercises again, or new ones you didn't do on the day? It is important to leave sufficient time before reviewing or you may become discouraged at the lack of movement.

➢ Don't neglect your on-going relationship with God. The Soul Workout is not designed to replace daily prayer times. If you already have a routine for personal devotions then continue with them. If you don't, then perhaps it would be helpful to look at introducing a regular pattern of prayer. After all, walking along the road and climbing the stairs are important ways to exercise and done more frequently than any gym workout. In the same way, a regular routine of scripture reading, prayer and meditation keep our spiritual hearts primed and pumping and no Soul Workout can replace that.

➢ If a small item, such as a pebble or a ribbon was used in your workout, you might find it helpful to carry it with you in a pocket or handbag: being able to touch it can bring reassurance and remind you that God is with you, no matter what you face. (If you were part of a group and don't have access to the items used, find something similar to carry with you as a reminder.)

➢ If you used any poetry on the day and found it helpful, then buy a book of poems (or ask for one as a present) to use in future prayer times. There are a few suggestions at the end of this book but go and browse in bookshops to get an idea of what might speak to you. You may also find rich treasure in reading the words of hymns out loud: coming from a Methodist background hymns have formed a part of my spiritual heritage. I no longer worship within a mainstream church but I am rediscovering the depth and insight contained within the traditional hymns I used to sing (and all too often without proper regard for what the hymn writer was saying). I am often surprised by how these old hymns speak into my situation. New worship songs are also important here so don't discount them—and they may be easier to get hold of. Try them and see if they hold a treasure for you.

➢ *At the end of the day it can be helpful to take a look back at how things have been for you: in Ignation spirituality this is called the **Review of the Day**:*

Think about the day: what you have done, where you have been, who you have seen. Let the day unfold in your mind without making any judgements about it. Having 'rewound' to the start of the day again you are now ready to review it . . . .

Firstly, consider what have you found to be energising or where you have felt close to God during the day. Acknowledge these things thankfully. Even on the hardest of days we can often detect some small thing that has helped: for example, it may be as simple as your spirits being lifted for a moment when the sun came out from behind a cloud or when a stranger smiled at you as you passed. It is so easy to discount or ignore these passing things but they can be signs of God's presence with us, if we can but see them.

After reviewing these 'consolations' (as Ignatius describes them) then take another moment to acknowledge the more difficult aspects of your day: those times where you felt drained of energy, dis-spirited or where you felt there to be some kind of barrier between you and God. Try not to make any judgement calls about these things but merely make note of them, asking God for His love and blessing. Sometimes it is in these times of 'desolation' (as Ignatius calls them) that we begin to yearn more for a deeper faith and a stronger sense of 'God with us'. In retrospect we often find that these are the times of growth when our faith *is* deepened and our spirits *are* strengthened.

But in a daily review it can be hard to see beyond the struggle!

After a few minutes of reviewing in this way I find it helpful to say a simple prayer to ask God's protection and provision for the night ahead.

➢ *A variation on the above suggestion is to spend a few minutes reviewing the day with the following questions:*

What three things have I enjoyed or appreciated today?

What one thing have I not enjoyed or appreciated?

Have I have seen anyone today who made me feel appreciated or special?

Have I told someone today how special they are and how much I appreciate them?

Is there anything I want to say to God about these things?

> If you sense that you need to talk with someone about your spiritual walk, then you may consider looking for a Spiritual Director (also known as 'Spiritual Companions' or 'Spiritual Accompaniers'). If you are unsure how to access information about Directors in your area then looking online will give you some ideas or make enquiries through your local parish church. Most Anglican and Catholic Dioceses hold information about directors in the area and some will also advise on how to look for the right person for your needs. Even if, like me, you do not belong to either of these traditions you will still be able to use this facility: many and varied are the people who make use of Spiritual Direction. See **Appendices 2 and 3** for further information about Spiritual Directors in Britain.

> You may feel that you would benefit from making a retreat from time to time. There are many retreat centres throughout the country—indeed, throughout the world! Information can be obtained online—look for 'Retreat Association'. An annual 'Retreat Journal' is also produced and lists information about many retreats taking place across the country.

Soul Workout

If you can't get hold of a copy easily through a Christian bookshop then your newsagent may be able to order it in for you.

➢ Have you thought of joining with like-minded people from time to time to further explore and deepen your spiritual life? The best way to find out is to ask around in different church networks, or look online: Contemplative Fire is a national organisation (google the name for information) and may be of interest to you but there are other groups throughout the country. If you can't find anything to suit, why not start something yourself?

➢ There are many online sites offering daily prayers and meditations: again I have included one or two I am familiar with in Appendix 2. There are many more.

➢ Reading books can be helpful in deepening our understanding of the spiritual life. You must already have some interest in this area or we wouldn't be having this conversation! There are literally thousands of books written about the Christian faith. Not all will appeal to you—you might even find some offensive. Look for authors you enjoy, ask friends what books they have read or look for book reviews. Try reading widely but use books as thought provokers and not as absolute truths—after all, books are only the written thoughts of another imperfect human being (including this one!).

➤ The wonderful thing about all of this is that God loves you unconditionally. You don't have to DO anything or BE anyone special to be loved by God. His love is a completely free gift. Take hold of it with passion.

Postscript

My hope is that Soul Workout will have offered new ways to experience God, encouraging spiritual awareness and a way of deepening the soul journey. If I have succeeded in any of these objectives then my own hard work of writing this book will have been more than rewarded.

AND FINALLY....
A WORD OF THANKS

I cannot end without acknowledging the help I have received from many quarters in the concept of Soul Workout and in the writing of this book.

Thanks to Christine Dodd with whom I had the initial discussion about the metaphor several years ago and who helped me on its debut outing as a Quiet Day at Whirlow Grange. I am also grateful to the people who have participated in the days and given me invaluable feedback on how it worked for them.

In the writing of this book I want to record my thanks to Adrian and Wilma Scott, Janet Morley, Anne Brien and Hazel Coates for reading the drafts, offering constructive suggestions and giving their support in many different ways.

Thanks also need to go to the fitness instructors and members of the gyms I have attended over the years: their names go unmentioned but without them and the experiences they have provided me with, this book would have gone unwritten and the metaphor unrecognised.

I particularly want to thank my husband John, my daughters Alison and Cheryl, and my son-in-law Dave for being such a close, loving family: you have always been there for me in the ups and downs of life and without your encouragement I would never have pursued my dream to write.

Thanks also to Kay, my friend and colleague at Footprints Connection, for encouraging and supporting all my mad ideas at work and for living the vision alongside me.

Life is a journey we share with so many; 'thank you' to all who have shared something of their journey with me.

Appendix 1

Suggested programmes for Soul Workout Group Events.

Full day programme

9.30-10.00 *Registration* (may include time for coffee)

10.00 *Welcome, Housekeeping notices and general outline of the day*, including making people aware of areas to be used as 'stations' *see Chapter 3 for further tips.

10.15 *Introducing the metaphor*: general overview and Explaining the Warm Up and Cardiovascular modules
*taking the metaphor for both at this point allows for a smooth transition into personal work at the end of the warm up.

10.45 *Warm up exercise* (group)

11.15 Time for *Cardiovascular* exercise: individual work using stations—if possible, arrange for group members to have access to drinks as / when they wish.

Soul Workout

12.30	LUNCH
1.15	Re-assemble as a group: introduce the *Weight Resistance, Flexibility and Balance* metaphors: *expanding on both together allows people to decide their own transition time from one exercise to the other.
1.30	*Preliminary exercise* (individual work but done within the group space)
1.50	*Time to lift those weights!* Individual work using stations, followed by the transition into personal work on flexibility and balance—if possible, arrange for group members to have access to drinks as / when they wish.
3.15	Re-assemble as a group for the *Cool Down* exercise. Final notices / handouts from PART THREE
3.45	CLOSE

Half day programme (3 hours)

9.15-9.30	*Registration*
9.30	*Welcome, Housekeeping notices and general outline* of the session—including making people aware of areas to be used as 'stations' *see Chapter 3 for further tips.
9.45	*Warm up exercise* (group).

10.00   *Introducing the metaphor*: explaining a Cardiovascular workout (metaphor)
10.15   Time for *Cardiovascular exercise*: individual work using stations—if possible, arrange for group members to have access to drinks as / refreshments when they wish or have 10 minute break before the exercise begins.
11.40   *Re-assemble together*: EITHER move into 'Listening Groups' of 3 or 4 people to share whatever is wished from the exercise (note: these are not discussion groups but a chance for each person to speak and be heard by others, without comment or judgement). OR use the time to expand the metaphor, even though there will be no time to follow up with exercises—this may be an opportunity to sound out the interest in a follow-up session.
12.00   *Cool Down* Exercise (group).
12.15   CLOSE

Evening programme (2 hours)

7.00   *Registration* and Welcome
7.15   *Brief explanation of the metaphor* as a whole followed by a more in-depth look at the module for the evening: this can be EITHER Cardiovascular OR Flexibility and Balance.

Soul Workout

7.40	*Brief Warm up* exercise (group).
7.50	*Exercises* from the chosen module (individual).
8.45	*Re-assemble for a Cool Down* exercise (group).
9.00	CLOSE

APPENDIX 2

Suggested Reading

- Margaret Silf 'Sacred Spaces' published by Lion (2002) a look at Celtic sacred spaces to see what they say to us in our faith journeys

- Henry Morgan and Roy Gregory 'The God you already Know' published by SPCK (2009) explores different ways of praying. A wonderful section devoted to the stories of people who have met God through their interests and in their pain.

- Anthony de Mello SJ 'Sadhana: A way to God' published by Bantam Doubleday Dell (paperback 1978) a classic book teaching different ways into meditation through eastern tradition—these methods are valuable as a Christian contemplative way of praying.

- Gerard Hughes 'God of Surprises' published by Darton, Longman and Todd 1985 another classic in the Ignation tradition. Ways into contemplative prayer show us that God is, indeed, a God who surprises us with His love.

- Richard Rohr 'Everything Belongs: the gift of contemplative prayer' published by Crossroads Publishing (1999). Relying on God as the source of all good things—even when the going is tough.

- Rob Bell 'Velvet Elvis' published by Zondervan (2007)

- Rob Bell 'Love Wins' published by Collins (2011)

  Both of these books by Rob Bell will take you on a journey of looking afresh at God's deep love for us. Some will find his conclusions controversial—but read with an open mind and be prepared to fall in love with God once again.

- Adrian G. Scott 'The Call of the Unwritten' published 2010; available through Amazon or directly from Adrian at www.adriangscott.com

  A collection of poems about life; written from the heart.

- Pat Marsh 'Silent Strength' published by Inspire (2005), available through Amazon

A collection of poems delving into the joys and burdens of life and faith

- Liz Babbs 'The Celtic Heart' published by Lion Publishing plc (2003)
  'The Pilgrim Heart' published by Lion Hudson plc (2006)
  'The Restful Heart' published by Lion Hudson plc (2006)

Each of these books of poems, reflections and quotations comes with a CD of reflective music, suitable for use during a Soul Workout event.

- Liz Babbs 'Celtic Treasure' published by Lion Hudson plc (2009)

A collection of poems, prayers and reflections of Celtic spirituality, including brief histories of Celtic saints and their treasured prayers

- The Bible Reading Fellowship (BRF) publishes a variety of books, journals (including 'Quiet Spaces') and Bible reading notes, including 'New Daylight'; 'Guidelines'; 'The Upper Room' and 'Day by day with God'. These can be purchased through Christian bookshops or at their online shop at www.brfonline.org.uk

- 'Retreat' is the Retreat Association (UK) Journal, published once a year and is available from most Christian bookshops or can be bought online from the Retreat Association website: www.retreats.org.uk

This publication gives information about retreats across the country along with useful articles for those thinking of making a retreat.

Resources Online

(This information is correct at the time of writing in July 2013)

www.sacredspaces.ie	This site, run by Irish Jesuits, offers daily prayers and meditations using scripture. These can be accessed while online or printed for use at other times. A good resource when personal motivation is running low.
www.rejesus.co.uk	Offers daily prayers and meditations on scripture. Once on the site, just follow the links to the daily prayer section. This site offers a lively place to learn about the Christian faith and spirituality.

www.annunciationtrust.org.uk	As well as offering suggestions and ideas for creative prayer this website gives information about Spiritual Direction and finding a Spiritual Director.
www.soulspark.org.uk	Information is offered about Spiritual Accompaniment (Direction)—how to find an Accompanier and what to expect in meeting with your Accompanier. Information is also given about the Soul Spark course and booklets.
www.retreats.org.uk	Information about Spiritual Direction, how to use it and how to access it is given alongside information about retreats.

APPENDIX 3

Seeking Spiritual Direction in Sheffield, South Yorkshire and North Derbyshire

(This information is correct at the time of writing in July 2013)

Footprints Connection: jointly run by myself and Kay Gilbert; we offer an eclectic range of spiritual direction (both), Quiet Days (both), counselling (Kay), Art & Soul open meetings (both), Art & Soul Workshops (Janice)

Contact us at: Footprints Connection
Carterknowle Methodist Church
Edgedale Rd
Sheffield
S7 2BQ
Telephone 0114 2587495
Email: footprintsconnection@gmail.com
Website: www.footprintsconnection.org.uk

Soul Workout

Whirlow Grange Spirituality Centre, holds names of Spiritual Directors in the surrounding areas of South Yorkshire and the Peak District of North Derbyshire. The centre also offers a wide variety of Quiet Days, conferences and retreats.

Contact: Whirlow Grange Christian Spirituality Centre,
Ecclesall Rd South,
Sheffield, S11 9PZ
Telephone 0114 2353704
website: www.whirlowgrange.co.uk/spirituality

END

About the Author

In 1989 Janice Speddings set up Footprints Counselling Service with a few colleagues in Sheffield, England. She believed God had called her out of social work and into a ministry of counselling—a belief that has stood the test of time: Footprints is still offering its services in 2013. Over the years it has evolved into Footprints Connection and now includes, amongst other services, one-to-one spiritual direction and group events such as Art & Soul.

She is also part of a team offering Quiet Days at Whirlow Grange Spirituality Centre in Sheffield.

As an experienced counsellor, spiritual director and group facilitator Janice Speddings has all the right credentials to write this Soul Workout book, but it is no dry, academic tome on spirituality.

Her style of writing is down-to-earth, sometimes humorously anecdotal but always with a serious message behind it.

Soul Workout

The practice of attending to and developing a deeper spiritual awareness of relationship with God, others and self is one she is passionate about and is the reason for Soul Workout.

Unafraid to become vulnerable to her readers, Janice Speddings offers us the chance to be honest and real about our own struggles by being honest about hers.

She is married to John and has two adult daughters, a son-in-law and a cat. Her hobbies are reading, writing, arts and crafts—and trying to stay fit.